MAKING METAL CLAY JEWELLERY

Julia Rai

THE CROWOOD PRESS

First published in 2017 by
The Crowood Press Ltd
Ramsbury, Marlborough
Wiltshire SN8 2HR
www.crowood.com

British Library Cataloguing-in-Publication Data

A catalogue record for this book is available from the British Library.
ISBN 978 1 78500 264 9

Frontispiece: Pod earrings with enamel and pearls. (Photo: Paul Mounsey)
All photographs are by the author except where credited otherwise

DEDICATION
I would like to dedicate this book to my Mum who has provided endless support and encouragement to me throughout my life, through all my ups and downs and has always been there when I needed her. I would also like to thank my family and friends for their support over the years. Finally, I would like to thank all my students. Every time I teach a class, I learn something new and I have always considered it a privilege to introduce this magical material to people, especially those who think they are not creative. I hope people reading this book will discover their creativity using the medium of metal clay.

Typeset by Kelly-Anne Levey
Printed and bound in India by Replika Press Pvt Ltd

CONTENTS

INTRODUCTION

I first discovered silver metal clay while attending a weekend course in silver jewellery making for beginners which I took as a birthday gift to myself in 2003. I have always enjoyed creative pursuits and thought making silver jewellery would be fun. On this course, the tutor was talking about this new medium called precious metal clay. I was intrigued and took a metal clay course soon afterwards. That was the beginning of my relationship with metal clay, a relationship which has taken me in directions I would never have dreamed of in that first course.

I took as many classes as I could in the first few years after discovering how much fun metal clay was to work with. I discovered a supportive and sharing community in my fellow metal clay adventurers and travel to the US became an annual pilgrimage to the conferences which ran each year. I began teaching metal clay in 2007 and have taught regularly both in my home county of Cornwall as well as around the UK since then. In 2008 I joined the only credential programme for metal clay artists, the Masters Registry, and began submitting pieces for the five level programme. I was the first person in the world to achieve level four which is where I currently sit alongside only one other person. I am working on level five and continue to support other artists who are on the programme via a Facebook page I set up specifically for this purpose. Introducing people to metal clay is

my passion and seeing their faces when they create something beautiful in solid silver never gets old.

Metal clay was invented in Japan in the 1990s. Two main brands emerged at that time; Art Clay Silver, made by Aida Chemical Industries and Precious Metal Clay, or PMC, made by Mitsubishi Materials Corporation. They both launched a fine silver version of the clay – 99.9 per cent pure silver and Hallmarked as fine silver, 999 – and at that time it required a kiln to fire it. The main target audience for metal clay was people working in ceramics so they already had kilns. It was launched outside Japan in the mid-1990s and once a torch fireable version was made available, the medium reached a much wider audience.

Original formula Art Clay was followed by Art Clay Silver 650 which required a lower firing temperature and made the clay torch fireable. This variety also had a slow dry version, Art Clay Silver 650 Slow Dry, which provided users with a longer working time for the clay straight out of the package. In 2014 Aida launched new formula clay which combined the properties of both their 650 clays and this became simply Art Clay Silver, their only fine silver clay variety.

PMC Original was Mitsubishi's first clay and was discontinued in 2013/14. The first torch fireable PMC brand was PMC+ which was comparable with Aida's torch fireable version. PMC3 is the most popular of Mitsubishi's clays. It is the strongest of the PMC branded fine silver clays when fired in a kiln.

The silver used in these clays comes from recycling silver used in a number of industries including dental, photographic and jewellery

Art Clay Silver and Precious Metal Clay (PMC) are the main brands of silver clay.

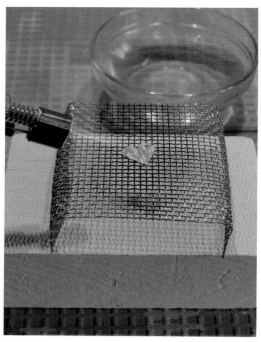

Torch firing small pieces is quick and easy.

making. This makes silver clay a completely recycled product and gives it green credentials which are important to many people in the modern world.

The development of metal clay since the launch of the fine silver version has been phenomenal. Fine silver clay in lump, paste and syringe form has been available for the longest time. Both main manufacturers invented a 22ct gold version of the clay, as well as a gold paste version early in the development of the medium. They also both have a sheet or paper type of clay which has quite different working properties to the lump clay.

In 2008, a bronze and copper version of the clay was invented by an American company and although these clays required a kiln to fire them, the reduced cost of the clay made this an attractive medium for artists and jewellers. Since then, other brands of silver, bronze, brass, iron, copper and steel clay have been developed in Europe, the USA, Canada, Australia and Japan.

Both Aida Chemical Industries and Mitsubishi Materials Corporation have continued to develop their silver brands and refine their product ranges. Aida launched Art Clay Copper in 2009. Mitsubishi launched PMC Pro in 2010 which is a mix of silver and copper and very strong. This proved less popular than their other clays, especially in the UK, as it did not easily fit into the Hallmarking categories being 90 per cent silver and 10 per cent copper. Mitsubishi followed this with the launch of PMC Sterling silver clay in 2011 which appealed to jewellers looking for stronger silver clay than the softer fine silver. It was also easy to Hallmark as 925 which is widely recognised by consumers. They launched PMC Flex in 2014, which is silver clay with a longer working time than PMC3 and the ability to remain flexible after the clay is dry. Flex has a PMC3 base but contains additional ingredients that make it flexible after drying. Artists working with these clays have also combined different varieties to create hybrid clays, for instance the so-called 960 hybrid which is a combination of equal quantities of PMC Sterling with PMC3, PMC Flex or Art Clay Silver.

This book is only covering making jewellery using fine silver clay from the two main brands, PMC and Art Clay. These clays are simple to fire and are very reliable. Some of the base metal clays and the newer silver clay brands require more complicated firing processes and can be more problematic for those new to the medium. Although PMC and Art Clay are made by different manufacturers, the working properties and firing schedules are very similar so whichever brand is used, the information and projects in this book will work. The references to metal clay throughout this book will be generic and will encompass PMC+, PMC3 and Art Clay Silver unless otherwise stated.

The medium of silver clay has been likened to alchemy and the feeling of magic in action is hard to escape. It is so accessible; it can be worked with on any kitchen table with simple and cheap tools, and the ability to torch fire it makes it available to a very wide audience. The learning curve is quite gentle, so people who work with polymer clay or even fondant icing, can easily work with silver clay. Imagine being able to design a pair of earrings and make them in a morning to wear that evening. That is what metal clay provides; the ability to realise unique designs, quickly and easily.

This book will cover making a wide range of jewellery using silver clay in the form of lump clay, paste, syringe and sheet or paper type. Join me for a journey of discovery with this amazing medium.

Brooch with punched hands and Oregon Sunstone. (Photo: Paul Mounsey)

WHAT IS SILVER METAL CLAY?

Types of Silver Clay

Silver metal clay has three ingredients, fine silver particles, an organic binder and water. The binder is proprietary to each manufacturer but it is non-toxic and both brands feel very similar when working with them.

Lump clay

The lump form of the clay in an unopened package will keep for years. Lump clay straight out of the package can be rolled out, textured, cut, hand moulded, extruded or pressed into a mould. The beauty of working with lump clay is that if what has been produced does not work, simply squash it up and start again. One of the biggest issues in working with lump metal clay is drying out. As soon as the lump clay is exposed to the air, the water begins to evaporate so being prepared before opening the package is crucial to working successfully with the medium.

Storing lump clay properly is also very important. It should be stored wrapped in cling film inside an airtight plastic bag or pot. Always spritz the clay with some water before storing it once work is completed. Spritzing some water in the bag or pot to create a moist atmosphere will also help to ensure the clay stays in good condition for the next time it is needed.

OPPOSITE PAGE: **Two main brands of silver metal clays.**

Lump clay.

Paste

The paste form of the clay is simply clay with more water added. Both manufacturers produce a paste form but it can easily be made by adding water to small pieces of lump clay in an airtight pot. The paste form is also sometimes called slip. This is a term used in pottery for watered down clay. Paste is used to stick pieces together, to add surface texture or effects and also to paint natural objects, like leaves.

If paste has been stored for a while, it can separate so stir it using a metal spatula before working with it. It can also dry out completely but can easily be rehydrated by spraying water onto the dry paste and mixing it until smooth. Keep it stored in an airtight container and always make sure the lid is tightly closed. If the paste starts to get a little too thick, add a few drops of water and stir well. Having several pots of paste available, each with a slightly different consistency, gives a good selection to add different effects when needed.

Art Clay has a silver clay paste especially formulated to adhere to glass or glazed surfaces. It is called Overlay Paste. It is useful to add silver decoration to fired and glazed pottery or porcelain, glass or to polished metal. It can also be used to fix cracks or splits in fired silver clay.

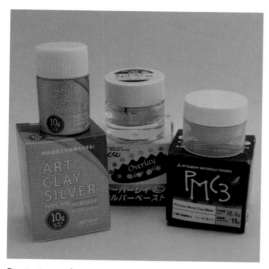

Paste type clay.

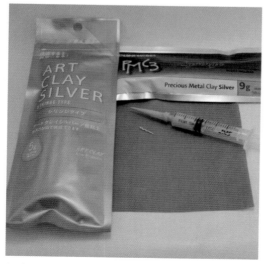

Syringe type clay.

Syringe

The clay is also available in the form of a syringe. This is paste which is specially formulated to extrude from the syringe nozzle and hold its round profile. Mastering the syringe comes more easily to those who have iced cakes using an icing bag and requires a steady hand to produce specific patterns. Syringe clay is used to add surface decoration to a lump clay base and can also be useful for adding paste precisely to a crack or gap in joined pieces of dry clay. Used over some form of supporting material which burns out during firing, it creates filigree effects in three dimensional objects. It can also be used to create open work designs inside a supporting frame of lump clay.

Syringes should be stored nozzle down in a pot of water. By keeping the tip of the nozzle under the water, the syringe clay does not dry out. Syringes kept in this way last for months, as long as the nozzle does not dry out. If it dries in the nozzle, it prevents the syringe from extruding smoothly and in extreme cases it can become a solid plug in the nozzle which has to be chipped out with a sharp tool. Any syringe clay which has become dry like this can be added to dry lump clay and reconstituted in the same way.

Paper or sheet

Paper or sheet type clay is produced by both manufactures and this is where each brand differs. Art Clay Paper type is very much like a sheet of thick silver foil. It is not wet, but metallic, and once opened, it does not require any special storage except to be kept dry. PMC Sheet has a PMC+ base but again, it is not wet. It feels very much like soft fabric and just needs to be kept dry to maintain its properties. Both brands come in two shapes, long and slim or square. Both paper/sheet brands are good for adding appliqué designs to the surface of dry lump

Paper and sheet type clay.

clay work. They can be cut with fancy scissors or paper punches to create interesting surface textures or patterns. They can also be woven by cutting strips and weaving them together with a tiny dot of water to stick them in place. Origami is another application which lends itself to using sheet or paper type clay.

Working Stages

There are three working stages with lump, paste or syringe metal clay; wet stage, dry stage and fired stage.

Wet stage

The first stage is working with the clay straight from the package while it is wet. In this stage, it can produce a completed form, such as a pair of textured earrings, or elements to join together when the clay is dry, like two halves of a bead. Syringe decoration can be added to rolled out clay or to a support of some kind, like a burn out

core of cork clay, wood clay or paper clay. Paste can be painted onto leaves or pods.

While the clay is wet, it is easy to texture and cut but it is more difficult to handle without squashing or damaging the edges. Finger print jewellery is made by impressing a finger or thumb into wet clay but if a piece has been textured using an interesting texture plate, putting finger prints into it will spoil the design.

The biggest issue working with wet lump clay is drying out. If the edges of the clay are looking cracked, it is probably too dry. To rehydrate clay which is getting a little dry, follow this process:

- **Take a sheet of cling film and put the clay into it**
- **Press it through the cling film, making it as flat as possible to create a large surface area**

Put a slick of water onto the flat sheet of clay inside the cling film.

Press the folded clay away from the fold.

- Spray water onto the work mat – not onto the clay – and using a finger, put a slick of water all over the clay surface, so it is glistening
- Fold the clay in half inside the cling film but handle it outside the cling film so the clay is not being handled directly
- Press the folded clay flat and away from the fold to avoid trapping air in it
- Open the cling film and fold the clay again, then repeat the pressing
- Continue to fold the clay and press it down five or six times

This process forces the binder to take up the water very quickly and will allow continued work with the clay. If this has been done correctly, there should be no wet clay on hands when it is picked up. Lots of clay on hands indicates that the clay is wet on the surface and has not fully absorbed the water.

Dry stage

The clay will naturally dry out if it is left open to the air. Small, thin pieces will dry in around forty-five minutes in a warm room but may take

A coffee mug warmer is a good way to dry your clay.

longer if the working environment is cold and/or damp. As the clay dries out, water evaporates and the piece will shrink slightly. The major shrinkage of the clay occurs during firing.

When the clay is dry, it can be easily handled without damaging the texture. This allows for joining pieces together or sticking wet clay elements to an already dry piece using paste. Paste can also be added to the surface of the clay to create texture effects and syringe lines can be applied for decoration.

In the dry stage holes can be drilled in the clay using a hand drill, contours can be filed into the edges, strips of clay can be cut with a sharp knife and edges can be refined with an emery board or file. Any dust that is produced from filing or drilling can be reconstituted or added to the paste pot to make more paste.

Dry clay is quite brittle and can break if handled too roughly. Clean breaks can normally be fixed with a little water or paste but if the break is bad, the dry clay can easily be reconstituted.

The clay must be completely dry before it is fired. If wet clay is fired, the water inside turns to steam and will burst through the surface of the piece, damaging the texture. In extreme circumstances, the piece can puff up like a pillow and make an almighty bang which can be very frightening. Always make sure the piece is thoroughly dry before firing.

Firing

During the firing process, the binder holding the silver particles together burns away leaving pure silver. This creates the main shrinkage of the clay. Art Clay Silver shrinks by about 10 per cent, PMC slightly more. This shrinkage needs to be taken into account when designing pieces.

Firing can be done by butane torch, gas stove or kiln. During firing a process called sintering takes place. Each tiny particle of silver sticks to its neighbour to create a solid silver end product.

RECONSTITUTING SILVER CLAY

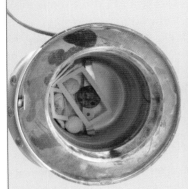

Store dry clay in a coffee grinder.

Dry clay dust.

Mix water into the clay dust to rehydrate it.

Dust turning to clay.

Turn out onto cling film.

Roll inside cling film.

Flap it over and keep rolling.

A kiln is a good investment.

The clay must be fired below the melting point of silver, which is 961°C/1762°F but at a high enough temperature for sintering to occur.

PMC3 and Art Clay Silver are classed as low fire clays. The lowest temperature that PMC3 can be fired at is 600°C/1112°F and for Art Clay it is 650°C/1200°F. The lower temperature firings are done in a kiln and apply to pieces which have glass or Sterling silver inclusions. Glass and Sterling cannot take higher temperature firings and glass needs to be slowly heated and cooled so is not suitable for torch or stove firing.

To get the strongest outcome, long and hot firing in a kiln is required. The recommended kiln firing schedule for purely fine silver metal clay pieces is 900°C/1650°F for two hours. This long, hot firing results in a dense, strong metal piece and is ideal for rings or for anything that needs to be extra strong.

PMC3 and Art Clay Silver can be fired with a butane torch or gas stove as this will allow for higher temperature firing. It is possible to melt fine silver pieces with a butane torch so care should be taken to ensure the piece does not get too hot.

If a piece is going to be torch fired, keep it small. The whole piece needs to be kept equally

hot and this is not possible if the piece is larger than 2.5cm/1 inch across. If moving the torch around is the only way to keep the whole thing hot, the piece is too big.

The torch firing process should always be done in a low light environment. The only way to tell if the piece is hot enough is by the colour of the metal so having a dimly lit room means the colour can easily be seen.

The torch firing process

Once the firing station has been prepared – see next chapter – the piece can be fired. Always wear safety glasses for eye protection when firing.

- **Adjust the torch flame to be bushy and gentle, not pointy and fierce**
- **Direct the torch flame at the piece, at an angle, not pointing straight down as this can result in the torch getting too hot from the heat rising up**
- **As the piece is heated, the first thing to be seen is the binder burning away. This will produce a flame which will burn briefly**
- **Next the metal will heat up and begin to glow**
- **When the metal glows with a salmon pink colour, begin timing with a three minute countdown timer**
- **When the timer goes off, turn off the torch**
- **The piece can be left to cool down naturally or picked up with tweezers and dropped into cold water to crash cool it**

Gas stove firing

Gas stove firing is very similar to torch firing except the piece is fired from underneath. Put a sheet of stainless steel mesh on the grid over the gas jets and turn on the gas. Allow the mesh to heat up and notice where the mesh glows,

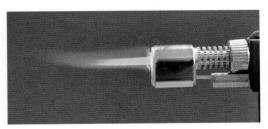

Bushy flame for firing.

The binder burns out first.

A pointy, fierce flame should be avoided.

A salmon pink glow means you are at the right temperature.

these are the hot spots. Turn off the gas and use tweezers to place the metal clay pieces where the hot spots were seen. Turn the gas on again. The binder will burn away first and when the pieces are glowing salmon pink, start the timing. Do not leave the pieces to fire; always stay with them until the time is up. Again, the pieces can be left to cool naturally or crash cooled in water.

Kiln firing

Buying a kiln is a major investment but for those who are are serious about working with metal clay, it is an essential part of the tool kit. Flat metal clay pieces can be placed directly on the kiln shelf. Anything that has a curved surface or is not completely flat should be cushioned somehow. There are two main ways of doing this; vermiculite and fibre blanket.

Vermiculite is a naturally occurring hydrated magnesium aluminium silicate mineral. After mining it is heated and this process produces particles of different sizes. It is very light, absorbs water well and does not burn. It is sold in garden centres and is mixed with soil to create a moisture retentive growing medium for plants.

As it does not burn, it is great for supporting curved forms. Place a pile directly on a kiln shelf or use a stainless steel or unglazed ceramic dish to contain the vermiculite. Nestle the pieces in the vermiculite and fire.

Fibre blanket is a ceramic fibre cloth which can be used to support pieces or can be wrapped around things to give them extra support. It can be used over and over again but care should be taken when tearing it up. Because it is made of ceramic fibres, these can get in the air and should not be breathed in. The more times fibre blanket is used, the crisper it gets and this can also produce particles of ceramic material if it is torn. Wear a dust mask to avoid breathing in the fibres.

Kiln firing allows multiple pieces to be fired at once and a good sized programmable hobby kiln – like the Paragon SC2 – can take two or three shelves of pieces in one firing. When buying a kiln shelf, remember to also buy the posts so shelves can be stacked on top of one another in the kiln. Kiln furniture kits normally consist of a shelf and four posts. Posts of different sizes can be bought which gives more flexibility for stacking shelves.

A kiln is essential when combining glass with metal clay. The two can be fired together but

Vermiculite and fibre blanket.

Multiple pieces can be fired in the kiln.

glass inclusions require a slow heat up and cool down cycle to avoid thermal shock, which would shatter the glass. A programmable kiln allows control of the rate of heating, called ramping, and it turns itself off so if the door is kept shut, it will cool down slowly too.

Programming the kiln allows control of the firing temperature with much more precision than torch firing allows. This provides more flexibility for the firing schedules used.

Potential firing issues

If an interruption occurs during the firing process begin timing again when firing resumes. It is fine to fire the pieces for longer than three minutes so if there is a break in the firing, it will not hurt to start the timing again from the beginning. In fact, the longer the piece is fired, the potentially stronger it will get.

Sometimes during the firing the salmon pink colour fades which means the piece has become cooler. To ensure the piece is fully sintered, when the timer goes off, continue to fire the piece for a while.

Fired stage

If the piece has been fired correctly, it should be matt white after firing. This white look is the natural surface of the silver. Examination of the fired metal under a microscope would show lots of hills and valleys which are the open pores of the surface. As the light hits the surface, it is dissipated making it look matt white. To flatten the hills and close the pores of the metal, burnishing is required and this is achieved using a brass or steel brush and an agate or steel burnishing tool.

If there are any silvery areas on the surface, the piece has slightly melted. This is normally seen during the firing process as a flash of silver across the piece which is the surface of the silver melting. If this happens, just pull away a little to cool the piece a bit but keep firing for the full three minutes. The worst that normally happens is a loss of the surface texture although occasionally, if a small element melts, like the leg of a star, that part may melt away into the main piece.

Occasionally, pieces can warp during firing. This could be due to the clay being stretched during the making process or stresses during the firing process, especially in pieces which have areas with different thicknesses. Flat pieces can be flattened by tapping them with a rawhide or nylon mallet, cushioned with a piece of leather or a wadded up kitchen paper to protect the piece. Gently tap it, turning it over a few times, until it is flat again.

Fired metal clay is just metal and can be treated in the same way as any other metal. It can be drilled, filed, hammered, dapped, soldered,

A matt white surface means you have fired it correctly.

Examples of melted pieces.

riveted, enamelled or have a patina added. Torch fired pieces can be prone to breaking if they are hammered too hard and metal clay prong settings that have been torch fired are generally not strong enough to stand up to the bending process. Kiln fired pieces are very strong though so if the design requires elements to be bent after firing, it is best to fire long and hot.

Two fired metal clay pieces can be joined together with thick paste and refired allowing all kinds of design possibilities. Any metal clay pieces can be fired multiple times if necessary. If a piece has been torch fired and subsequently there is a requirement to bend it, kiln fire it hot and long and it will be stronger.

Health and Safety

Silver metal clay is a safe product although it should not be ingested. Wash hands after working with the clay and before eating. It is good practice not to smoke or eat while working as metal clay will quickly pick up any ash or crumbs which are very difficult to remove. It will burn out during firing but may leave pits in the finished piece.

In the dry stage, the clay is refined by filing which produces dust, as does drilling holes in it. This dust is quite heavy and tends to drop easily but people with any lung issues should wear a dust mask to avoid breathing the dust in.

Torch or stove firing the clay is inherently dangerous as they require working with an open flame. Take these precautions:

- **Always tie long hair back**
- **Wear clothes which are non-flammable and avoid floaty sleeves, scarves or anything dangling**
- **Wear close toe shoes, just in case a hot piece gets dropped**
- **Keep full attention on the firing and avoid doing it when young children are around**
- **Do not look away from the piece while torch firing, looking away gives the potential for the piece to get too hot or too cold**
- **Keep a fire extinguisher handy and if possible a fire blanket**

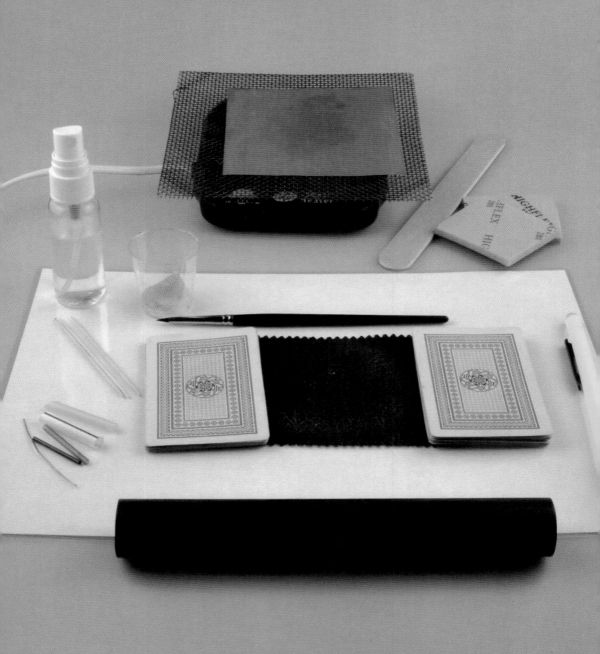

TOOLS AND EQUIPMENT

Metal clay is a material that requires very few tools. Like any medium though, there are multiple tools available, with new things coming out all the time. It is easy to be seduced by new tools but generally, there are a few tools which will be used over and over and these should be the first investment. They are also quite cheap which is a bonus. Having taught hundreds of beginners, very often they already have the basic tools from other things they do so it is always worth checking before buying anything new.

Wet stage tools.

Wet Stage Working Tool Kit

Work surface

A smooth, non-porous, wipe clean work surface will protect the table and also ensure the work area can be kept clean. Possible work surfaces include:

- **Plastic place mats**
- **A sheet of thick glass, like a glass chopping board**
- **Glazed ceramic tiles**
- **A laminated piece of card is also an alternative. For precision, a work surface which incorporates a grid is a good idea. This can be printed out onto thick card and laminated to create a bespoke work surface.**

OPPOSITE PAGE: **A basic work area set up.**

Release agent

As metal clay contains water, it can be sticky so it needs some form of release agent on work surfaces, tools and hands to prevent this. Many people use a commercial product called Badger Balm which is an organic hand balm made chiefly from olive oil and beeswax. A cheaper alternative is to use olive oil from the kitchen. Out of date olive oil that is no longer used for cooking is ideal and any vegetable oil will work. Avoid anything with a petroleum base, like Vaseline, as this reacts badly with the clay. There are also a few commercial products specifically made for use with metal clay but olive oil is the most accessible product for this.

Use any release agent sparingly on tools, textures, work surfaces and hands. Too much oil makes the clay hard to work with as it slips around. Over time, if clay is being reconstituted again and again, too much oil will undermine the clay. If it begins to get crumbly and no amount of water helps to make it workable, it has probably soaked up too much oil. Mix the contaminated clay with an equal amount of fresh, new clay to provide clay that is usable again.

Roller

The basis of most pieces of jewellery made with metal clay is a flat slab of clay. A smooth, non-porous roller will result in a good finish. This could be made of acrylic, plastic or glass and often people have something they could dedicate to their metal clay work. Acrylic plumbing pipe makes a good roller and offcuts can sometimes be found in the local hardware store. Or buy a length of pipe and cut it into pieces of around 20cm with a hacksaw.

Rolling guides

To ensure that the clay is rolled out to a consistent thickness, rolling guides need to be used. Acrylic spacers are available from all metal clay suppliers. These are strips of acrylic of different thicknesses which are placed on each side of the clay rolling area. The roller edges rest on the guides and the clay between them is rolled to the appropriate thickness.

A cheaper alternative to these guides is to use playing cards. An equal stack of playing cards each side of the clay allows rolling to a consistent thickness and also provides lots of control of how thick the clay is. A standard playing card is approximately 0.25mm thick so four cards are 1mm thick. Four cards or 1mm is the thinnest that the clay should be rolled to for making a simple, lightly textured piece, for instance a pendant or earrings.

If a heavy texture is used, like a rubber stamp, the clay will need to be rolled out thicker than this to prevent the texture from cutting through the piece. When attaching layers to a piece, thinner clay can be used for the layers, depending on the design. Using playing cards gives the freedom to roll the clay as thick or as thin as needed for the design.

The tutorials in this book will refer to playing card thicknesses.

Drinking straws

Drinking straws in a variety of sizes are useful tools to have. Very small ones will punch a hole in rolled, textured and cut out pieces for a jump ring. This is the simplest way to make a hole in the clay in the wet stage. Wrapping clay around a larger straw creates a bead or laying a straw between two flat pieces stuck together creates a channel for a chain or cord. Always make sure the plug of metal clay left in the straw is pushed out after use. A small piece of wire is useful to keep with the straws for this purpose and the plug can be put back with the excess clay.

Cocktail sticks

Cocktail sticks or tooth picks can be used to create texture, cut out free hand shapes and can also provide an armature to prop up bits of the design or put a curve into a flat piece. They are useful in the dry stage too as they can be used to clean out holes punched using a drinking straw.

Teflon

Teflon sheets are useful for transferring wet clay to the dryer. If clay has been rolled onto a texture, moving it onto a sheet of Teflon allows it to be put directly onto the surface of a hotplate to dry. Teflon can be purchased from supermarkets as it is used to line baking sheets.

Textures

Metal clay is made for texture and there are so many options. Texture is all around us and there are also many sources of commercial textures including rubber stamps, plastic and metal texture plates and heavy cardboard textures designed to be used in rolling mills.

Non-commercial textures

Carry a piece of polymer clay in a small sealed bag to test out textures when out and about. This will give a good idea of what the texture will look like but do be respectful of delicate finishes or fragile plants and so on.

Here are some good sources of non-commercial textures:

Wallpaper

Cheap or free, wallpaper is a great source of texture. Vinyl textured wallpaper will last the longest but even very cheap textured paper will last for quite a few uses. Visit a local hardware or DIY store and take a sample from the open packages. A little olive oil on the rolled out clay is needed when impressing non-vinyl wallpaper into it to avoid it sticking. Wallpaper will soak up oil very quickly so oiling the rolled out clay instead ensures it does not stick.

Natural objects

Leaves, nuts, dried plants, pods, bark and grasses can all make interesting textures. Waxy or solid leaves can be oiled as can pods. Bark may need to have the rolled out clay oiled before impressing. Be careful not to use something that sheds as this can result in small pieces being stuck in the clay and having to be picked out. Some grasses have seeds that stick in the clay and dry bark can be quite flaky. This is not a problem if

Natural items make great textures.

the whole piece that has been rolled is going to be used but if the piece is going to be cut after texturing, there may be bits of residue in the excess clay. Any bits of organic material in something that is going to be fired can be left, it will burn out, but it will need to be removed from excess clay that is going to be used again.

Skeleton leaves are great for texture and can often be used several times. They are available from hobby shops and there is also a UK supplier who only sells skeleton leaves, see the suppliers section at the back of the book. Always press the side with the most pronounced central vein into the clay. Oiling is not always necessary with skeleton leaves as they can easily be peeled out of the clay.

Shells have great texture and are very easy to use with metal clay. They often do not need oiling as they are quite slick and hard but if the surface is rough, use some oil to make sure the impression is clean with no sticking.

Feathers are fun to use, whether they are fluffy ones or solid ones. The fluffy type cannot really be oiled as this results in a loss of the fluffy nature of the feather but if the rolled out clay is oiled, the feather can be placed on the surface and rolled in. Try using the edges of more solid feathers to give an interesting effect.

Fabric, lace and button textures.

Buttons

Check out the button box or visit a local knitting or sewing store to see if they have some interesting textured buttons. Plastic, metal or resin buttons just require a light oiling to prevent sticking.

Haberdashery and fabric

While in the sewing store, have a look at the fabrics. Lace and ribbon are great texture sources as are fabrics like muslin or hessian. Oil the rolled out clay rather than the fabric before rolling.

Leather is a wonderful texture to roll out onto ensuring the back of the piece has a great texture too. Small samples of leather, even faux leather, can be easily oiled and have subtle, shallow textures.

Around the house

Texture is everywhere around the house, from bottle and tube tops to kitchen utensils. A tea strainer makes an interesting texture and screws, nuts and bolts can be impressed into the surface to make marks. Press the tines of a fork into the clay or roll a toothpaste tube lid across a rolled out sheet.

Hobby stores and craft shops

Hobby stores and craft shops are a rich source of potential texturing items. Angelina fibre, sometimes called angel hair, makes an interesting texture. It is designed to be fused by using a hot iron so it sticks together. This creates a sheet which can be sewn onto things or used in card making or other hobby pursuits. Ironed or not, it can be rolled into the clay to produce a texture.

Sequin waste – referred to as punchinella – is often sold in hobby shops in small sheets. It is what is left after the sequins have been punched out and makes a great texture. Common patterns are circles, stars and squares but shopping around uncovers other interesting shapes. As these are often metallic plastic, just a simple slick of oil is enough to prevent them from sticking.

Children's toys

Many children's toys have great textures. Check out the wheels of toy cars, plastic figures or space ships, bike reflectors or game pieces.

Making custom textures

There are many ways to make custom textures, some of which are quite technical and outside the scope of this book. A very easy way to make a texture is to carve into an eraser. Lino or wood carving tools or a simple craft knife can be used to cut pieces out of the eraser surface to create a texture. Pressing a ball burnisher or a ball point pen into the surface of thick watercolour paper creates an indent which can be impressed into the clay. This also works with pieces of clean Styrofoam, like the base of pizza packaging.

Commercial textures

There are many sources of commercial textures, some designed specifically for metal clay. One of the biggest issues with using a commercial texture is seeing the same textures used by other artists. Artists keen to use their own designs and especially those who are selling their work, need to use commercial textures creatively to avoid this.

Rubber stamps

Rubber stamps are a great source of texture for metal clay but they need to be used carefully. Rubber stamp mats, sheets or small hand held stamps are normally quite thick as they are designed to be used with inks to make a clean, crisp print on paper or card. Rolling a rubber stamp sheet or mat into the clay can be problematic if it is not well oiled or the thickness of the stamp has not been considered.

To really get oil into all the nooks and crannies of a deep and/or complex rubber stamp, use a paintbrush with the oil. Brush the oil into all the crevices of the texture in the place which will be pressed into the clay. Make sure the clay is rolled out thick enough to take the depth of the stamp. For a really deep texture, the clay will need to be rolled out about 0.5–0.75mm thicker than the stamp. Lightly pressing the stamp into the rolled out clay to get a shallower outcome also works but this can take a few goes to get right.

When using a hand held rubber stamp, the same considerations and precautions need to be taken but there is a little more control when pressing it down by hand. It can still take a couple of goes to get the desired result but it is worth it.

Plastic or metal texture sheets

There are a wide range of plastic and metal texture sheets available commercially with varying depths. Brass texture plates tend to be lightly etched and the textures are ideal for using on the back of pieces. Roll the clay out onto the oiled texture, making sure that the playing cards or rolling guides are sitting on the edges of the texture plate. This will ensure the correct thickness is being rolled.

Making your own textures is fun.

Commercial texture examples.

Plastic plates are mainly thicker than brass ones but not generally as thick as some rubber stamps. They are easy to oil and simple to use. If the plate is too big or the design requires a specific piece of it, just cut the sheet with scissors to make it more manageable.

Laser cut card textures

There are some low relief textures being produced that use laser cut card to create a pattern which is impressed into the clay. One supplier of these based in the US, Rolling Mill Resource (see supplier section), will create a custom design for a small fee. This can be really useful if producing unique designs is important. This supplier will also invert a design or make it larger or smaller to really custom-ise the textures that they have in stock.

Laser cut card textures can be used multiple times with metal clay if they are treated carefully. Oil the plate each time it is used. Because it is card, it will absorb the oil but this will not affect the tex-ture. Store the plates flat with something protect-ing the texture. A small plastic bag works well.

Cutters

Once the clay is rolled out and textured, the next step is to cut it into a shape suitable for the design. There are several ways of doing this. A craft knife, tissue blade or pin tool can be used to cut a free-hand shape. Stencils can also be used, as can commercial cutters.

Commercial cutters

Normally made of metal – steel or brass – cutters can be bought from all metal clay suppliers and also from sugar craft suppliers. There are several varieties of commercial cutter.

Cookie cutters

Small cookie cutters are available in two main qualities. Very cheap cutters are made of steel and are joined using a flap over method. This leaves a notch in the edge of the cut which needs to be dealt with after the piece is dry. They tend to have one cutting edge and one rolled over edge, making them one sided. This is not a problem for symmetrical shapes but asymmetrical shapes cannot be used to make a mirror image pair of earrings when these cutters are used.

More expensive cutters have soldered joins which cut more cleanly and they are also double sided so they can be flipped over to cut mirror images. These cutters often come in nesting sets of shapes which are a good investment. Having multiple sizes of the same shape is useful for making sets of jewellery, like earrings and a pendant.

Oil the cutting edge to achieve a clean cut. If the clay sticks inside the cutter, ease it out by gently pushing one corner or edge away from the inside with something rounded, like the end of a paintbrush handle.

Plunger cutters

These cutters usually come in brass or plas-tic. The brass kind are well made and have no seams on the cutting edge so make a good clean cut. The plastic ones normally have a less sharp and defined cutting edge but are still useful and can be cheaper than the brass kind. They sometimes come in sets, either graduated sizes of the same shape or a selection of shapes at the same size. The plunger is used to ease the clay out if it sticks in the cutter. These cutters still need to be well oiled.

Plunger embossing cutters

Embossing plunger cutters are mainly avail-able from sugar craft suppliers. They combine a

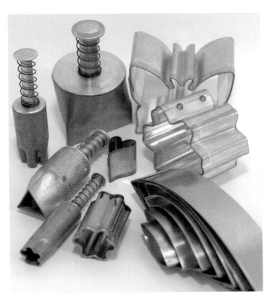

Commercial cutters.

Embossing cutters.

cutter with an embossing plunger part which textures the shape once it is cut. They are plastic. To use these, oil the cutting edge and the embossing surface. Roll out the clay and cut the shape. Before lifting up the cutter, push the plunger down firmly to emboss the surface of the clay. These embossing cutters can be very useful to produce multiple copies of the same thing.

Stencils

Another way to cut out a shape is to use a stencil. Commercial stencils are available from many suppliers and it is worth shopping around to find interesting shapes. These are used with a pin tool or craft knife. Oil the cutting tool and use it at a 90° angle to the clay to create a clean cut edge. Take care not to press the stencil down onto the clay too hard but make sure the clay is held in place for a clean cut.

Stencils are available in a wide range of shapes and sizes. It is useful to have a whole sheet of the same shape in different sizes, like graduated circles, ovals, hearts, squares or rectangles, as well as some more unusual shapes.

Selection of stencils.

Making custom stencils is easily achieved by cutting out the shape from thick card stock. Cereal packets are a good source of card stock. Draw the shape and cut it out using a sharp craft knife on a cutting mat.

Moulds

Pressing things into the clay will give a good impression but sometimes the design may require something more three dimensional or maybe the requirement is to capture the object as it appears in reality. Shells are a good example of this. When a shell is pressed into the clay, the result is a negative of the actual shell. Making a mould of the shell and pressing the clay into the mould results in the positive, the shell as it actually is in reality.

Moulds can be made using polymer clay which is baked to create a usable mould but polymer clay tends not to give the type of detail that can be achieved in other ways. It can also be quite inflexible although using a bake and bend polymer clay formulation can help with this. Two part silicone moulding compound generally gives a far better end result and will also create a flexible mould which is very useful. There are a number of brands available from the metal clay suppliers. Check the setting time of the silicone compound before buying. The ideal is something that gives a bit of working time in case the mould is not right first time. Some set very fast and do not give much time for reworking.

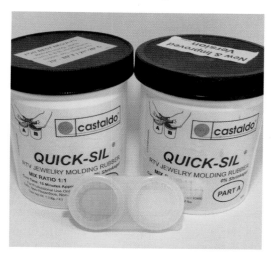

Two part moulding compound gives you superior moulds.

Mix equal quantities of each colour together until there is no more marbling of the colours. Create a smooth surface to the mixed compound and then place it down on a firm surface. Press the item into the compound until it comes up to the edge. Do not allow it to come over the edge or there will be an undercut which will prevent easy removal of the metal clay when using the mould. Leave the item in the compound until it sets. Test it using a cocktail stick; if the cocktail stick leaves a hole, it is not set. Silicone moulds do not need oiling normally although a very light slick of oil on the surface of the mould can be used if any sticking occurs. Use an oiled paintbrush to get into very complex moulds.

Commercial moulds are available online, often aimed at the sugar craft market and polymer clay artists but increasingly targeted at metal clay artists. While these are a great source of interesting designs, it is so easy to make moulds which allow for the creation of unique designs specifically tailored to the needs of the artist.

Opt for flexible moulds wherever possible when buying them to use with metal clay. Rigid moulds can be very hard to use as they cannot be flexed to eject the clay while it is still wet. Leaving the clay in the mould to dry is fine but there is no way of knowing if a good impression has been achieved until the clay is completely dry. This can slow down the production process and often moulds are not suitable for speed drying on a hotplate.

Commercial moulds also include double-sided moulds, allowing for three dimensional designs which are especially useful for creating earrings or charms.

Drying the clay

Speeding up the drying of the clay can be achieved in a number of ways. A small coffee mug warmer works very well when working at home. Put a piece of stainless steel mesh over the hotplate to make the heat less fierce. A hair dryer is also a useful tool, as is a food dehydrator. Any form of gentle heat will help the pieces to dry more quickly. They can even be put in a domestic oven on a low heat, no higher than 100°C/212°F.

Using Teflon sheet to transfer pieces to and from the drying source will prevent burned fingers as the metal clay can get very hot if it is in contact with the surface of a hotplate or in the oven.

Dry Stage Working Tool Kit

In the dry stage, there are a few tools which are needed. The simplest tool is an emery board. This is used to refine the edges of the dry clay and is especially important if cheaper cutters are used which leave the notch in the edge. Always file the edges of the clay over a clean, dry work surface so all the dust can be captured. This dust can be put with the other dry pieces for reconstituting or can be added to the paste pot to make more paste.

Sponge or foam sanding pads are a good investment. They come in a variety of grades and can be cut to size allowing access into tight spaces. They are good for refining curved surfaces.

Polishing papers are useful to create a mirror polish surface on any part of the piece. Work through the grades of papers from the harshest to the finest to create a super smooth surface before firing. This will make the mirror polishing done after firing much easier.

If a jump ring hole was not made with a drinking straw in the wet stage, drilling a hole in the dry stage with a hand drill is an easy alternative. Use a 1mm drill to create a hole 0.8mm after firing. The metal clay is soft enough to drill using the drill bit alone but it is more comfortable to use a pin vice or hand drill for this. Always start small when drilling a hole larger than 1mm. Drill a small pilot hole and then gradually enlarge the hole with larger drill bits. Support the piece from behind while drilling. A rubber block can be very useful for this.

Dry silver clay is great to carve into, using lino

Dry stage working tool kit.

or wood-carving tools. Draw the design on the surface of the clay with a pencil. The graphite will burn out during firing. Keep the carving tools at a low angle while carving and make the carved line deeper in stages.

It is in the dry stage that pieces are stuck together so a good quality paint brush is useful for adding paste and cleaning up any residue. Keep paint brushes clean and never allow them to stand in water for any length of time. Also do not stir paste with a paint brush. This will force paste up into the bristles of the brush and ruin it. Use a metal or plastic spatula to stir the paste.

Firing Tool Kit

For torch firing silver metal clay, protection of the work surface is the first priority. A large ceramic tile – like a floor tile – with a fire brick on top will prevent the heat from reaching the work top when firing in the kitchen. Firing bricks are available from metal clay suppliers but a house brick will work just as well.

Putting a piece of stainless steel mesh with the ends bent down to create a platform on top of the fire brick helps to raise the piece up and also provides air flow and heat distribution around the piece during firing.

A simple cook's butane torch is fine for firing. Make sure the torch locks on, preventing the need to hold the trigger for the whole three minutes. A torch with a piezo ignition is safer than having to light it with a match or lighter. Some torches have safety locks so the torch cannot be turned on by accident.

Use a countdown timer to time firings, do not guess the time. Choose a timer with one handed push button start and stop as starting the timing happens once the piece reaches the correct temperature.

Tweezers are needed to pick up the piece once it is fired and drop it into cold water to crash cool it, known as quenching.

Firing station set up.

Mesh bent at the ends to create a platform for firing.

Fired Stage Working Tool Kit

After firing, the piece is metal so normal metal working tools can be used to work with the piece. Useful tools to have are a rawhide or nylon mallet to gently tap pieces flat if they have warped during firing. Brass and/or steel brushes are used as an initial polishing tool after firing and a steel or agate burnisher is a good investment to give a high shine to edges and high spots of texture.

Adding findings like jump rings and ear wires require pliers and it is useful to have several pairs including chain nose, snipe nose or flat nose pliers. To make custom bails which are riveted to metal clay pieces, round nose pliers are useful to achieve a smooth bend in wire for the bail. A wire cutter is also useful. Often these tools come in a set which is a good investment. Buy really good quality tools and look after them well to ensure they last a lifetime.

Power tools are also useful when working with metal. Drilling holes in fired pieces using a bench drill is really quick and easy. Hand-held micro tools are a good investment and get a bench workstation, like a drill press, so the micro tool can be used

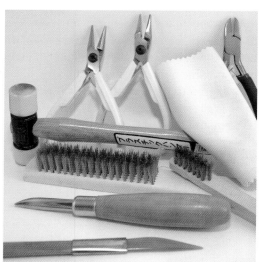

Metal working tools.

like a bench drill. Accessories for a micro tool include silicone polishing wheels and radial bristle heads which are great for achieving a high shine on silver.

Impregnated polishing cloths give pieces a final lustre and silver polish can be used to add the finishing touch.

TOOLS FOR SPECIFIC TECHNIQUES

Some techniques require specific tools.

Radial brushes are great for polishing.

Ring making

Ring mandrels are necessary to build a continuous band ring. These are normally wooden and it is useful to have a stand of some kind so that both hands are free to work with the clay while creating the ring.

An alternative to buying a ring stand is to use the edge of a food bowl to suspend the mandrel. Use lumps of polymer clay or BluTac to provide anchors on each side of the bowl holding the mandrel steady while you work. You can also make a stand using bent wire – like coat hanger wire – embedded in a piece of wood for the base. Bend two pieces of wire into M shapes using your mandrel as a guide for how deep and wide the central V needs to be. Drill holes the same size as the wire at each end of a wood block to create a home-made stand.

A ring sizer is essential and can be purchased very cheaply. A plastic ring sizer is fine. Check whether the sizer has UK, US, Japanese or European ring sizes before buying and also if it includes half sizes.

A steel triblet with ring sizes marked along the length is a good buy. This is useful when making rings to order and also comes in handy if the ring warps slightly during firing. Use a nylon or

Ring-making tools.

Anchor the mandrel to a bowl with polymer clay.

rawhide mallet to reshape the ring on a steel triblet after firing. It is also used to bend open band rings after firing.

Armatures and supports

There are lots of options for making dimensional, domed or hollow forms. Drape wet clay over light bulbs, ping pong balls, marbles or other curved objects so it dries in a domed shape. Two domed shapes joined together with paste make a hollow form. Look out for things around the home that can be used to create different dimensional effects when the clay is draped over it. As long as the item can be easily oiled, is non-porous and can be made stable, it will work as a support for metal clay.

Examples of armatures and supports.

Create concave jewellery inside curved forms.

As well as doming pieces by draping them over a form, pieces can be put inside a curved form to create a concave shape. This works well for things like flowers where the design requires the flower to curve outwards. More complex forms with built-up petals or embellished central areas, like sunflowers, can be created using this method.

Pieces can also be built around an armature that burns out. Cork clay, wood clay and paper clay are good examples of this. Make sure they are fully dry before building pieces around the armature.

Polymer clay cannot be used as a burn out core as it is plastic and produces toxic fumes when it burns. It can be used to create unique forms for laying silver clay over and drying though. Mounting it on a pencil also provides a useful handle to move the form around when creating the metal clay piece. Form the shape in polymer clay around the end of a pencil, bake it following the manufacturer's instructions and then oil it and lay the silver clay over it to dry.

Build clay around a polymer clay form and remove before firing.

Stone setting

Faceted stones that can be fired in place are easy to set directly in the wet stage just by pushing them into the clay or using a drinking straw or small brass tube to cut a hole in the clay for the stone. A more elegant way of setting faceted stones is to make a hole for the stone in the dry stage.

A setting burr or appropriately sized drill bit will make a cone-shaped hole in dry clay into which the stone can be set. A range of drill bits is required in progressively larger sizes. Small drills 0.8mm–1mm create a pilot hole and then larger drills enlarge the hole and create the cone shape until it is big enough to accommodate the stone. Setting burrs do the same job but can be slower than using a drill. They are slightly more controllable though, so are useful for people who are less confident using a drill bit which tends to cut the clay more quickly.

A set of drill bits is a good investment and they often come in a holder so you can keep them in size order. You can also buy setting burrs in sets for setting different sized stones. Although you can use the drill bits or setting burrs in your fingers to drill the hole, a hand drill or pin vice makes it easier when using smaller drill bits or burrs. There is no need to use a power tool when drilling holes in dry clay and you have more control by using a pin vice or just using the larger drill bits and burrs in your fingers.

Stones that cannot be fired in place will need to be bezel or claw/prong set. Stones can be set in a bezel using a burnisher to push the edge of the bezel over the stone. This can also be used to push prongs onto the stone. A bezel rocker and a grooved end pusher for claw/prong setting are useful when setting stones on a regular basis. Care should be taken to avoid slipping with any of these tools and scratching the stone, particularly softer stones which are normally bezel or claw set.

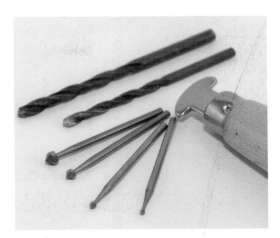

Stone setting tools.

A set of drills is a good investment.

WORKING WITH LUMP CLAY

This chapter explores working with lump clay to create a pair of earrings and a pendant.

Topics covered in this chapter include rolling out the clay to a consistent thickness, texturing both sides, working with asymmetrical forms, cutting with a cookie cutter and a stencil, drying, refining, firing, polishing, adding findings and dealing with breakages.

QUIRKY HEART EARRINGS

These earrings show the use of asymmetrical shapes in earring design. Earrings should be a mirror image pair and double edged cutters are perfect for this.

Tools and Materials

- 7g silver metal clay
- Sterling silver ear wires
- Textures for the back and front
- Double sided quirky heart cutter
- Small drinking straw
- Teflon sheet
- Cocktail stick
- Sponge sanding pad

1 Lay a piece of leather down on the work surface and put a stack of ten playing cards on each end of the leather. Lightly oil the leather, the roller, the drinking straw and both edges of the heart cutter. Choose the texture to use on the front of the earrings.

1. All ready to roll out the clay.

OPPOSITE PAGE: **Pendants and earrings using lump clay. (Photo: Paul Mounsey)**

2. Roll out the clay to four cards thick and then texture.

3. Make a hole in each heart.

4. Transfer the hearts to Teflon.

2 Roll out the clay, removing two cards at a time and turning the clay around before each roll to create a rolled out shape large enough to cut two heart shapes from. When the clay is four cards thick, lay the oiled texture onto the surface of the clay and with one roll, impress the texture.

3 Cut both hearts out from the textured clay, flipping the cutter before cutting out the second heart giving a mirror image pair. Remove the excess clay and wrap it in cling film. Take the drinking straw and cut a hole in the largest lobe of each heart. Remove the excess from the straw and put this with the other excess clay.

4 Carefully transfer the hearts to a piece of Teflon. The easiest way to do this is to flex the leather, raising an edge of one of the hearts. Slide the Teflon under the edge and transfer it without pressing on the clay. Do the same for the other heart. Allow to dry on a hotplate.

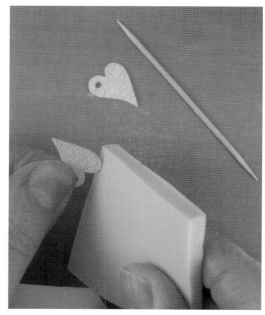

5. Refine the edges with a sanding sponge.

5 When the hearts are dry, use a soft sponge sanding pad to refine all the edges and clean the hole with a cocktail stick. Fire each heart separately for three minutes using a torch or kiln fire. Allow to cool or quench in cold water.

6 Polish the hearts using a brass brush in soapy water or a steel brush and burnish the edges with a steel burnisher. Hang the hearts on ear wires.

6. Burnish the edges.

PENDANT

This pendant uses a stencil for the main shape and has a cut-out design which saves on clay and creates interest. Choose a shape for the cut-out design that complements the main shape.

Tools and Materials

- 7g silver metal clay
- Sterling silver jump ring
- Chain
- Textures for the front and back
- Stencil
- Pin tool
- Small cutter
- Small drinking straw
- Teflon sheet

1 Lay a piece of leather down on the work surface and put a stack of ten playing cards on each end of the leather. Lightly oil the leather, the roller, the small cutter, the drinking straw and the pin tool. Choose the texture to use on the front of the pendant.

2 Roll the clay out to four cards thick, turning it around as two cards at a time are removed

1. Set up your work area and make your choices.

2. Roll and texture the clay.

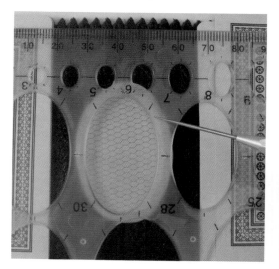

3. Cut out the stencil design with a pin tool.

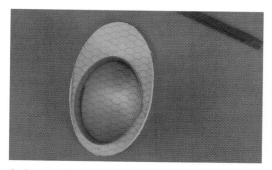

4. Cut out the central design and the jump ring hole.

making sure the stencil will fit. Texture the front of the clay and then lay the stencil gently over the rolled out clay and resting on the cards.

3   Hold the clay steady and using the pin tool, cut out the stencil design. Keep the pin tool completely upright and against the edge of the stencil. Before cutting out the other hole, transfer the stencil design to Teflon.

4   Transferring the piece to the Teflon keeps the shape when the central hole is cut out. Cutting the hole before it is transferred causes the shape to lose its integrity. Cut out the hole and make a hole for the jump ring. Put it to dry.

5   When it is dry, refine it inside and outside. The outside can be refined using an emery board on straight sides or a sanding sponge if it is curved. The inside edges can be refined using a cocktail stick or a small file. Remember to refine the jump ring hole. Fire the piece and then polish it.

5. Refine the inside edges with a cocktail stick.

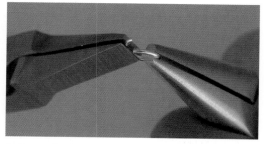

6. Open the jump ring by twisting it sideways.

6 Use two pairs of pliers to open the jump ring by twisting it sideways. This puts less stress on the metal and ensures the jump ring closes accurately. Hang the pendant on a chain.

Troubleshooting

Breakages

Pieces with a cut out can be prone to breaking more easily than solid pieces but sometimes pieces will also break around the jump ring hole, especially if the hole is very close to the edge.

Clean breakages on textured pieces can normally be fixed using just water. Wet both edges and on a flat surface, hold them together firmly for a minute. Carefully transfer the piece to a hotplate, being careful not to bend it, or leave it to air dry. If the breakage is not clean or the texture makes the break obvious, break the piece up and rehydrate.

Textures for the back

Rolling the clay out onto a texture automatically adds texture to the back of the piece. This means that the back will always be well finished and avoids spending more time cleaning the back before firing. Not every texture is suitable for use on the back of a piece though. Always choose a shallow texture. If the back texture is deep, there is a danger of making the piece too thin. The back texture also needs to be something that can be easily oiled. Choose plastic or metal texture plates or leather, which makes a great back texture. Vinyl wallpaper can also be used for the back but avoid regular wallpaper as it soaks the oil up and causes sticking. Avoid lace or other fabric for the same reason.

Pendant and earring set.
(Photo: Paul Mounsey)

Porous textures

Very porous textures, like regular wallpaper, fabric or lace, can be very hard to oil. In this case it is best to oil the rolled out clay before it is textured. Roll the clay down to four cards thick and then lightly oil the whole surface of the clay. Lay the texture over the surface and roll to impress the texture.

Metal clay brooch with acrylic sheet inlay.
(Photo: Paul Mounsey)

WORKING WITH SYRINGE-TYPE CLAY

This chapter looks at the syringe both as a stand-alone source of silver clay and combined with lump clay as a surface patterning method.

Topics covered in this chapter include: choosing and creating different nozzle sizes; good technique; correction of lines; random versus definite lines; working to a pattern; ensuring structural integrity: using embeddable, fire-in-place findings; supported structures and burn-out cores; adding syringe clay to dry pieces and drilling holes in the dry stage.

PATTERNED PENDANT

This pendant combines a flat back piece made from lump clay with a pattern added using the syringe.

Tools and Materials

- 5g silver metal clay
- 5g silver clay syringe
- Shape cutter/stencil
- Hand drill and 1mm drill bit

1   Roll out a back panel four cards thick which is textured on the back but plain on the front with no holes. Cut out the shape, transfer it to Teflon and put it somewhere warm to dry. Once it is dry, dampen the surface with a paintbrush and before the water is dry, use a finger to add a subtle stippled texture by patting the surface all over. Dry.

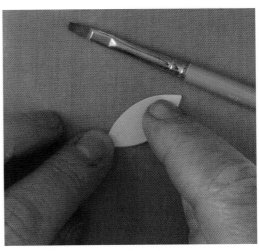

1. Add a finger stipple pattern to the surface.

OPPOSITE PAGE: **Jewellery made with syringe clay. (Photo: Paul Mounsey)**

2. Draw the syringe design on the surface.

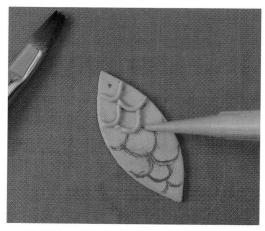

3. Build up the pattern gradually.

4. Drill a hole for the jump ring.

2 Draw the syringe pattern on the dry surface of the piece with a pencil. The pencil lines will burn out during firing. Remember to make the lines about the same size as the syringe nozzle and also factor in where the jump ring hole will be drilled. Plan that all the lines to be added to the surface do not cross over each other, as this can make the lines less solidly attached. Lines should butt up to other lines or can stand alone.

3 Dampen the surface where the syringe lines will be placed using a paintbrush. Add the syringe lines following the pattern. Correct any lines which deviate from the pattern using a damp paintbrush to nudge them into place. When the pattern is complete and dry, fill any gaps and smooth the lines. Dry the pendant and once it is dry, refine the edges.

4 Drill a hole using a hand drill. Support the pendant from behind during drilling by placing the pendant on a flat surface or putting a finger behind the piece where the hole will be. Do not put any pressure on the drill, let the cutting edge of the drill do the work and just turn it steadily until it goes through. Fire the pendant in a kiln or by torch. Polish as normal and add a jump ring to complete the piece.

OPENWORK PENDANT

This pendant uses open syringe work to create a free-form shape. It requires a steady hand with the syringe and also shows how to alter the size of the nozzle to ensure structural integrity of an openwork piece.

Tools and Materials

- 5g silver clay syringe
- Pencil
- Thick marker pen
- Wide transparent adhesive tape
- Playing card and paper

1   Take some time to design the piece. In order for the openwork design to have structural integrity, the lines will need to be at least 1mm thick after firing. They will also need to touch each other at multiple points rather than be hanging in space. Think about how the pendant is going to hang. With this technique, syringe loops can be made or hooks formed for jump rings to be added after firing.

2   Cut the end of the syringe nozzle so it is the same width as the lines of the design, somewhere around 1.2mm–1.5mm thick. Draw the final syringe design using a thick marker pen with lines the thickness of the syringe nozzle. Attach the design to a playing card using wide clear adhesive tape. Syringing will be done directly onto the tape.

3   Syringe the design following the pattern and using a damp paintbrush to nudge any lines into place as necessary. Butt lines up to each other, do not cross lines over. Parts of the design may need to dry before continuing to prevent damage to the lines already extruded. When adding fresh syringe to dry areas, dampen the touch point with water first to ensure a good join.

1. Design your piece on paper.

2. Prepare the syringe and the pattern template.

3. Syringe the lines following the pattern.

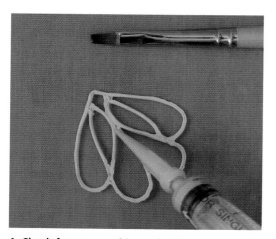

4. Check for gaps and imperfections.

5. Add a jump ring and hang on a chain.

4   Check the surface back and front for rough areas or gaps between joined syringe elements when the piece is complete. Fill any gaps with a smaller syringe nozzle, really getting into any spaces. Gently sand any rough areas using a sanding sponge. An alternative is to add a stipple texture all over the surface using a little paste on a stiff paintbrush.

BURN-OUT CORE MATERIALS

There are several types of materials which make good burn-out cores for metal clay. Cork clay, wood clay and paper clay are all easy to use and will burn out completely once fired.

Cork clay is a dense material which comes in a tightly sealed package and is damp and malleable. It burns out in the firing leaving the metal clay form built around it. Cork clay cannot be rehydrated so it needs to be stored in an airtight bag with some damp kitchen paper wrapped around it. Spritz some water into the bag before sealing it to make a moist atmosphere. Double bagging it will help to keep it in good condition and it should last a very long time.

Wood clay can be bought ready-made or in a powder form which is mixed with water. The powder form allows mixing of the exact quantity needed so there is less potential waste as the ready-made clay can dry out over time.

There are various brands of paper clay so be careful to buy a brand which burns out. Some brands include volcanic ash which means the clay does not burn. This type is good to make anything needed as a support during firing but should not be used with anything that encloses the paper-clay form. Paper clay is light and is normally usable straight from the package. *Papier maché* powder can also be used to make burn-out cores.

As cork clay comes in slabs, it is easy to use cutters to cut shapes for designs directly from the slab. To make two matching weight/size forms – like earrings – use cutters to cut out the clay and then form these into the shapes

5 Fire the piece by kiln or torch and polish gently with a brass brush in soapy water or a steel brush. Burnish the high spots with a steel burnisher on the inside and outside areas. Add a jump ring and hang on a chain.

needed. When using wood and paper clay it is best to weigh the clay to get equal quantities when making matched pairs. Break off pieces and form them into shapes by hand.

Any burn-out core must be completely dry before it is used with metal clay. Building something around a form that is still damp results in the water inside turning to steam during firing and causing the piece to explode in the kiln. It is best not to try and speed up the drying by using heat as this can dry the outside but not the inside of the form. Allow twenty-four hours drying time for a walnut-sized piece, longer for larger or thicker pieces. If in doubt about whether it is dry, leave it for longer.

Stick a cocktail stick into the core while it is wet and stand it up in a blob of polymer clay to dry. The cocktail stick forms a handle to hold the piece as it is worked on. When making beads, push the cocktail stick all the way through where the bead holes will be.

Ideally, a piece built on a burn-out core requires a kiln to fire. As it burns it produces flames and smoke so it is not generally suitable for torch firing. Very small pieces may be torch fired but this needs to be done out in the open and safety precautions should be taken. Anything with a burn-out core should be slowly heated in the kiln, called ramping. Programme the kiln to ramp at around 800°C/1470°F per hour so the burn out of the core is slow and gentle. Fast heating can cause the core to burn too hot and fiercely, causing collapsing of the metal clay around the outside.

Wood and paper clay make good burn out cores.

FILIGREE EARRINGS

These earrings use a random syringe pattern over a burn-out core of cork clay. Fire-in-place embeddable eyelets are used in this design. The earrings can only be kiln fired.

1. Two cork clay forms ready for drying.

2. Join the syringe clay to the tail of the eyelet.

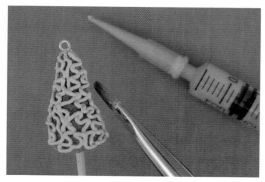

3. Random syringe pattern.

Tools and Materials

- 9g or 10g silver clay syringe
- Embeddable eyelets x 2
- Cork clay, wood clay or paper clay
- Cocktail sticks
- Small amount of polymer clay
- Good quality paintbrush

1   Make two identical forms using a burn-out material like cork clay, push a cocktail stick into each one at the bottom of the design and stand them up in a blob of polymer clay to dry. Allow at least twenty-four hours for them to dry completely.

2   Make a small hole in the top of each form and put the tail of the embeddable eyelet into the hole, leaving about 2mm standing proud from the surface. Extrude some syringe clay so it is touching the tail of the eyelet on one side and draw a random line a little way down the form. Repeat this on four sides of the eyelet tail.

3   Holding the cocktail stick in one hand, extrude the syringe lines in a random pattern all over the surface of the form, making sure the lines touch and cross over each other. Check often to make sure that there are no points sticking up or pieces not touching. Gently tamp down any stray pieces with a damp paintbrush but be careful not to flatten the lines.

4   Extrude the syringe pattern all the way down the cork forms while still keeping the form upright. Avoid turning the form upside down at this stage. If it drops off the cocktail stick it will damage the syringe design in which case

4. Only syringe part way down the form.

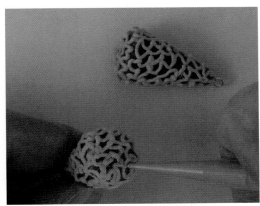

5. Syringe the base of the earrings.

it will need to be removed and done again. Stand the cocktail stick in the polymer clay to allow the syringe lines to dry.

5   When the lines are dry, it is safe to turn the piece upside down to complete the bottom of the form. At this stage the cocktail stick can be removed and the form can be held or placed in a crater of polymer clay. Do not push it into the polymer, this may dislodge the embeddable eyelet and damage the syringe work.

6   Make sure there are no big gaps or long areas where there is no syringe line. When all the syringe work is complete and dry, it is ready for firing. Create a nest of fibre blanket to nestle the forms. Kiln fire using a ramp speed of around 800°C/1470°F per hour, rising to a temperature of 900°C/1650°F and fire for two hours. This will make the final earrings stronger.

7   Check the integrity of the earrings and make sure the eyelets are firmly attached. At this stage, if there are any gaps or if the eyelets are loose, add some syringe and fire again. Gently brass brush the earrings in soapy water and burnish the high spots. Add ear wires.

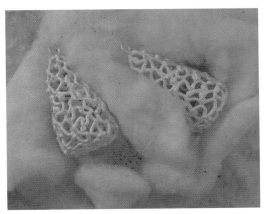

6. Nestle the forms in fibre blanket for firing.

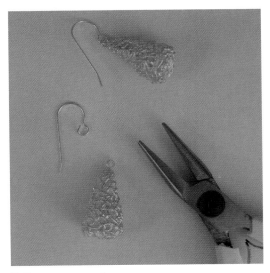

7. Hang on ear wires.

Troubleshooting

How to hold the syringe

This varies between people. Some like to hold the syringe like a pen and push the plunger with the other hand, others like to hold the syringe in their fist and extrude with the thumb of the same hand. Work out what works best by experimenting before starting the project. Try out various ways of working with the syringe by extruding lines onto a work mat. Any syringe which is extruded can be added to the paste pot or if it is dry, it can be reconstituted with the other lump clay.

Holding the syringe like a pen.

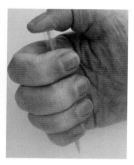

Holding the syringe in your fist.

Flat lines

If the lines are extruded with the tip of the syringe touching the surface, this can result in flat, uneven lines. Start a line by touching down but then lift up a couple of millimetres and allow the syringe line to drop from the tip of the nozzle. This will give a round line and also allows some control over where the line goes. To stop a line, touch down again and lift up quickly. If a point of clay is formed

when lifting up, use a damp paintbrush to remove or tamp down the point. With practice, this technique gets easier.

Thin or stretched lines

Lines become thin and/or stretched if the syringe is moved faster than the clay is emerging from the tip. Keep up a steady, consistent pressure on the plunger and move at the same pace as the clay is extruding.

Firing burn-out cores

Sometimes when a burn-out core is used, there is a residue of ash inside the piece. Run the piece under the tap for a while and this should remove any residue. Poke out any residue left using something thin and sharp like a cocktail stick or piece of wire.

Always fire the piece long enough for the core to burn out completely. This is not a technique to use if quick firing is required as slowing the heat up of the kiln is essential to avoid hollow forms from collapsing, especially open work forms.

Thin and stretched lines.

Flat syringe lines.

Examples of Jewellery Made with Syringe-type Clay

Pendant and earrings
with syringe decoration.
(Photo: Paul Mounsey)

Openwork syringe pendant.
(Photo: Paul Mounsey)

WORKING WITH PASTE-TYPE CLAY

This chapter looks at paste-type clay. It is useful to add texture to the surface of dry silver clay pieces and can also be used as multiple layers to build up a form.

Topics covered in this chapter include exploring the thickness of paste for different texture effects and painted leaves. Making a bail out of silver clay is also covered.

PAINTED LEAF PENDANT

Leaves with interesting shapes and good vein structures are popular choices for jewellery. While leaves can be rolled into the clay like any other texture, this technique is used to make light and strong natural looking jewellery. It retains all the natural bends or curves of the leaf in a way that rolling the texture in does not.

Tools and Materials

- A fresh leaf
- 10g-20g silver clay paste
- A good quality paintbrush
- Small spatula

1   Choose a leaf with a good shape and vein structure which is not too hairy, thorny or waxy. Make sure it has a good length of stalk as this will act as a handle when painting the leaf. When using new, fresh paste, take a small amount out of the pot using a spatula and put it onto a non-stick surface. Add a small amount of water to the paste so it is the consistency of single cream. Fresh paste tends to be too thick for the first few layers.

1. Choose the leaf and water down the paste.

OPPOSITE PAGE: **Pendants featuring paste.**
(Photo: Paul Mounsey)

2 Holding onto the stalk and with the leaf flat down on a clean surface, paint the underside with the paste, moving from the centre to the outside of the leaf. Make sure to cover the whole surface. Pick up the leaf by the stalk and move it away from any paste which has gone

2. Paint the underside of the leaf.

3. Five layers of watered down paste.

4. Use thicker paste to build up layers

over the edge onto the work surface. Leaving it in place results in the excess adhering to the edges of the leaf and spoils the shape.

3 Allow the layer to dry naturally; do not use heat to speed up the drying. If the leaf is exposed to heat at this stage, it is likely to begin drying out and curling up, causing the paste layer to crack. Use more watered down paste for the next four layers, allowing each layer to dry completely before adding the next.

4 After adding five layers of paste to the leaf, begin using thicker paste to add bulk. Be careful not to drag the thicker paste over the leaf as this can cause the existing layers to come away. Push the thick paste out from the centre of the leaf to the outside rather than painting it on. This is also now the time when gentle heat can be used to speed up the drying but avoid putting the leaf directly onto a hot plate.

5 Continue to add thicker layers until the leaf is around 1mm thick. Pay attention to the centre vein of the leaf which tends to stand proud from the rest of the leaf. The paste over this vein should be as thick as the rest.

5. Clean any blobs from the underside.

When the leaf is fully dry, check the underside – the side with the leaf on – for any blobs of paste. Leaving these in place will result in them firing to the front of the leaf and spoiling the texture. They can normally be gently removed with a fingernail.

6   Drill a hole for a jump ring and then fire using a torch or kiln. The leaf will burn away so it does not need to be removed before firing. Brush the leaf back and front to bring out the shine and add a jump ring. Hang on a chain.

PIERCED PENDANT WITH A SILVER CLAY BAIL

This pendant uses two different thicknesses of paste for the texture on the back and the front of the piece, a self-made stencil template and a metal clay bail. The natural white surface of the clay post firing is used as a feature of this pendant.

Tools and Materials

- 15g silver metal clay
- Thin and thick silver clay paste
- Paper and scissors
- A fine pin tool
- A flat piece of acrylic
- Drinking straw
- Teflon sheet
- Very small needle files
- Cocktail stick

1   Create a paper template for the pendant. Cut out a 5cm square of paper. Fold the square in half diagonally and then fold it in half again giving a smaller triangle. Fold each side of the triangle into the centre making a long dart shape with two points at the bottom. Cut the points off in a curved shape. Cut 'V' or curved shapes into the sides, top and bottom. Unfold the paper every so often to check the design.

2   When the design is finished, roll out the clay five cards thick directly onto a piece of oiled Teflon, making sure it is the right size and shape for the template. Lightly oil the paper template and lay it onto the surface of the clay. The oil will help it to stay in place but will also release the paper when the design is done. Use the fine pin tool to cut out the

1. Create a paper template for the pierced design.

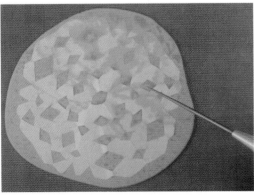

2. Lay the template on the surface of the clay.

3. Make a bail with a sausage of clay.

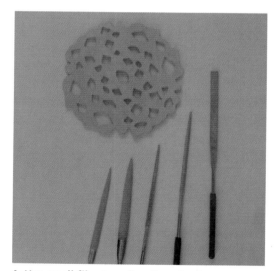

4. Use small files to refine the piercing.

5. Use thick paste to texture the front.

design, removing the inside elements as well as the outside edges. Remove the paper template from the surface and dry the piece.

3   While the piece is drying, make the bail. Take a small amount of clay and roll it into a short sausage shape. On an unoiled surface – use a flat piece of unoiled acrylic such as a CD case – roll the sausage into a longer, thinner snake of clay. Drape this snake of clay over a drinking straw so if forms a wide 'U' shape. Suspend it over a small cup and allow it to dry.

4   When the main piece is dry, refine all the edges, inside and outside. This is quite fiddly and the piece is also very fragile so take extra care and support it well while it is being refined. Very small needle files work well for this. It is also a good time to refine the outside shape from the original pattern template to make the design more pleasing if necessary.

5   Use very thick paste to add the texture to the front of the piece. The frosty effect on the finished pendant is achieved by leaving the deep areas of the texture white while shining up the high spots so it requires the texture to be thick. Paint sections of the front with thick

PASTE THICKNESSES

It is useful to have several paste pots with a range of thicknesses available. Vary the thickness of the paste by adding more dry or wet lump clay to it or by adding more water. For painted leaves, it is best to use fresh, pristine paste direct from the supplier rather than paste made from dry filings. Often filings and bits of dry clay contain foreign bodies like hairs, dust or crumbs and this can make the paste lumpy. This is not a problem when making a thick, random texture on the surface of a piece but it can be a nuisance when painting a leaf.

paste and then drag a cocktail stick through the paste to create deep score marks. Allow each section to dry before moving on to the next section.

6   When the pendant is dry, take the dry bail, lay it down on a cutting mat and use a sharp knife to cut the ends off to create an appropriately sized bail. The ends need to be straight and in line so file if necessary. Dampen the area for the bail on the back of the pendant and use thick paste to stick the bail on. Allow this to dry and then apply a paste texture to the back using the same method as the front but using thinner paste.

7   When the whole pendant is dry, check if any refining needs to be done to clear off any stray paste from the texturing. Fire the piece in a kiln or by torch, face down so the bail is sticking upwards. This will prevent the piece from warping during firing. Brush the back of the piece but just use a burnisher on the high spots of the front and the edges resulting in a frosty white finish contrasting with the high shine.

6. Stick the bail to the back of the pendant.

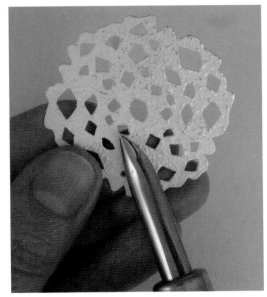

7. Burnish the high spots in contrast to the frosty white in the dips.

Troubleshooting

Leaves split

If the paste has been added too thinly over the central vein, the leaf can split down this area after firing. Make sure to really pay attention to the amount of paste being added to the central vein area and do not paint the paste off this area.

If the leaf splits in any other area, it is probably because the paste has not been applied evenly. Anywhere the paste is thinner will be weaker and more prone to splitting.

Wet paste pulling away from itself on painted leaves

Waxy leaves, like holly, do not take paste well. The paste tends to pull away from itself leaving gaps. Keep on dotting them in but this can cause problems with the integrity of the final leaf. Spraying the leaf with cheap hairspray creates a slight 'tooth' on the surface which can help with this issue. Avoid waxy leaves if at all possible for best results.

Tiny air bubbles

Leaves with hairs on the back can trap air and this causes tiny bubbles in the surface. Try to avoid hairy leaves if this is a problem.

Examples of Jewellery Using Paste as a Significant Element

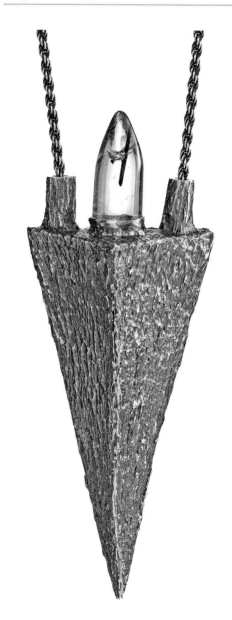

Hollow form necklace with paste texture and rutilated quartz cabochon. (Photo: Paul Mounsey)

**Pendant textured with paste.
(Photo: Paul Mounsey)**

WORKING WITH PAPER/SHEET-TYPE CLAY

Working with paper or sheet-type clay is very different from working with the clay in its wet forms and presents some interesting options which will be explored in this chapter.

Topics covered in this chapter include using paper punches and fancy scissors to add appliqué effects to the surface of lump clay pieces and creating origami forms by folding the sheet-type clay.

CICADA ORIGAMI EARRINGS

Cut out a 6mm square sheet of paper and practise folding this design before making it in the PMC+ sheet. The more times the folding is practised in this simple design, the better the final earrings will be.

Tools and Materials

- 2 x 6mm x 6mm square PMC+ sheet
- Hand drill
- Ear wires

1   Lay the PMC sheet on a flat, dry surface. Fold the sheet in half diagonally. With the point at the top, fold the base corners up to the point to create a diamond shape.

2   Fold down the points of the corners which were folded up in the previous step.

3   Fold down the top point of one layer, about a third of the way up the top triangle.

1. Fold the base corners up to the point to create a diamond shape.

OPPOSITE PAGE: **Jewellery made with paper-type silver clay. (Photo: Paul Mounsey)**

2. Fold the top points down on both sides.

3. Fold down the top point about a third of the way up the top triangle.

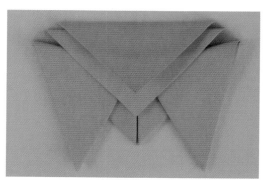

4. Fold down the second layer to create a chevron shape.

5. Fold the two sides behind to create the final shape of the cicada.

4　Fold down the second layer, making the fold slightly above the previous one. This creates a chevron shape.

6. Bend the earrings down the middle.

5　Fold the two sides behind to create the final shape of the cicada. Bend the overall shape in half down the centre so the piece has a bit of dimension. Make the second earring in the same way. These can be torch fired but they are very thin and light and can melt easily so kiln firing is preferable. Support the dimensional shape using fibre blanket under the bend.

6　Gently brush the fired earrings with a steel or brass brush to polish them. Bend them down the centre over the edge of a rubber block to accentuate the shape. Use a hand drill to put a hole in the top of each earring and hang on ear wires.

APPLIQUE PENDANT

This pendant uses a combination of lump clay and Art Clay Paper Type clay to create a surface design which is stuck onto the dry base. Embeddable bails are a useful addition to any toolkit and this project explains how to use them.

Tools and Materials

- Art Clay Paper Type metal clay
- 5g lump metal clay (any brand)
- Small amount of syringe clay
- Paper punches
- Fancy scissors
- Embeddable, fire in place bail
- Carving tool or craft knife
- Kitchen paper

1. Roll out the clay onto a piece of leather.

1　Roll out the lump clay five cards thick onto a piece of leather so the back of the pendant is textured but leave the front smooth. Cut out the shape of the pendant using a cutter or a stencil. Put the cut out pendant to one side to dry.

2　Practise the design using paper before cutting out the shapes using Art Clay Paper Type. When the design is finalised, cut and punch the shapes and lay them out on a dry surface.

3　Refine the edges of the dry pendant using an emery board. Turn it over and draw a straight line down the exact centre of the pendant with a pencil. Bails are best applied in the top third of a pendant form so they hang correctly. Mark the position of the top leg of the bail, lining it up along the central line so the bail is straight.

4　Take a carving tool or craft knife and dig out a small channel just large enough for the top leg of the embeddable bail. Keep checking the size of the channel with the bail. This channel only needs to be a millimetre deep so the bail leg is held firmly. When the first

2. Practise your design in paper.

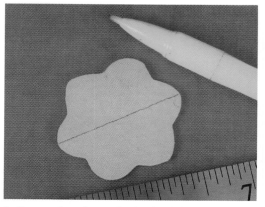

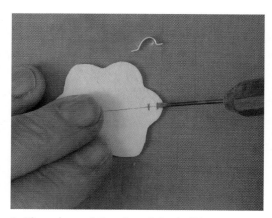

3. Draw a line down the back of the pendant to position the bail.

4. Dig a channel the size of the bail leg.

TIPS ON USING PAPER PUNCHES WITH METAL CLAY SHEET

Paper punches are a great source of shapes to be used for appliqué and allow artists to create multiple identical shapes quickly and easily. There are a wide range of micro punches available which are great for using with paper or sheet type clay. There are also larger punches which are made up of multiple small elements and these can be useful too.

Art Clay Paper Type is rigid enough to slide into the punch slot but PMC+ sheet is softer and more like fabric, making it tricky to control in the slot. To make it easier to use with paper punches, fold a sheet of tracing paper in half and trap the PMC sheet inside. This makes it easier to see where the cut is being made and also gives the sheet some rigidity, making it easier to handle.

Economic use of the paper/sheet type clay can be difficult so here are some tips to help make this easier. Turn the punch upside down so the cutting hole is visible and the punch plunger is down on the table. Slide the paper type or sheet in its tracing paper jacket into the slot to see exactly where to make the cut. Notice the edge of the clay or the previous punched shape and line the punch hole up so the cut is close to the previous cut edge, reducing waste. When the clay is in place, press down firmly exerting even pressure over the whole punch, so the shape is cut out cleanly.

Turn the punch upside down to see where you are cutting.

Prolonged use of paper punches with metal clay can blunt the punch cutters so the life of paper punches is less than would be expected if they were only used with paper, so bear this in mind.

Punched shapes can be used either way around, making asymmetrical shapes quite versatile. When using punched asymmetrical shapes on earrings, flip the punched shape to achieve a mirror image in the design.

Due to the nature of sheet or paper-type metal clay, punched shapes will keep forever as long as they are stored in a flat, dry place.

Remember too that the negative space created when a shape is punched out can also be a useful component in appliqué designs.

channel is done, mark the position of the other leg of the embeddable bail and dig out a channel for this one too.

5   Dampen the channels with water and squirt a small amount of syringe clay into each channel. Push the bail legs into the channels. The syringe clay will come up over the edges of the channels so smooth and clean this up with a damp paintbrush so the embedding is neat. Allow the bail to dry.

6   Place the pendant onto a piece of folded kitchen paper with a dip for the bail to sit in. This cushions the pendant and avoids damaging the embedded bail. Apply the punched and cut appliqué design to the surface using a very small amount of water between the sheet/paper type and the surface of the pendant. Allowing each element to dry before adding the next may be necessary if the design is complex. As only a small amount of water is being added to stick the pieces together, the drying time is very quick, especially if a heat source is being used.

7   When the design is complete and everything is dry, fire the pendant by torch or in the kiln. Brush, burnish or tumble polish the fired pendant.

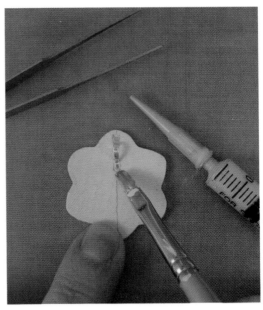

5. Embed the legs of the bail in the back of the pendant.

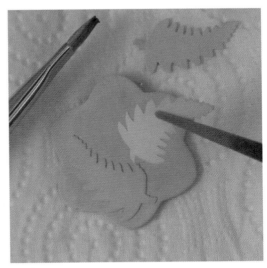

6. Use a small amount of water to stick the PMC paper shapes onto the pendant.

Troubleshooting

Too wet

The sheet and paper-type clays are very sensitive to water and if too much water is applied, they become mushy and break down. It is almost impossible to reposition a piece of sheet/paper-type when it has been wet and applied to another surface so take extra care when placing designs. If the sheet/paper type becomes mushy, allow it to dry and use it as surface texture. This can create some interesting, organic types of texture.

Cracking

The Art Clay Paper-type is like thin metal. If a hard crease is put in this type, it can crack so it is less suitable for precise origami designs that require hard creases. Once it has cracked, it cannot be stuck together again and is best put into the scraps pot for use in another project.

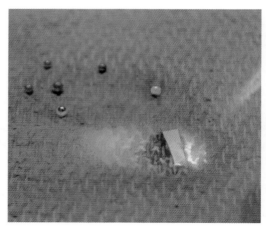

Melt offcuts of sheet or paper-type to form balls.

Offcuts and scraps

Offcuts and scraps are a common outcome when using the sheet/paper-type clays. These offcuts can be useful for making organic surface textures. Another use for them is to create fine silver balls for use in other designs. Cut them into small pieces and put on a charcoal block or firing brick. Torch fire them until they melt. As they melt, they form perfect silver balls which can be kept and added to unfired clay pieces using paste.

Examples of Jewellery Using Paper or Sheet-type as a Significant Element

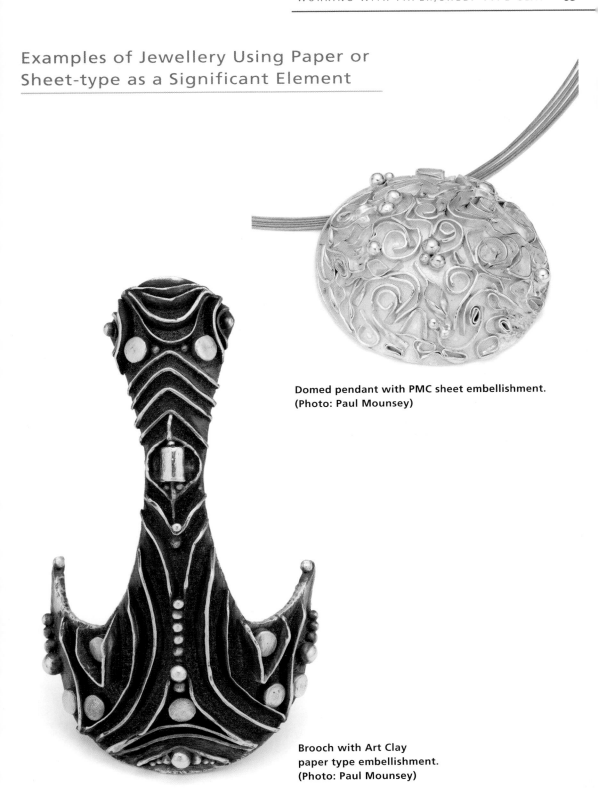

Domed pendant with PMC sheet embellishment.
(Photo: Paul Mounsey)

Brooch with Art Clay
paper type embellishment.
(Photo: Paul Mounsey)

MOULDING AND FORMING

The use of moulds with metal clay opens up a wide variety of options for jewellery items. From moulded components to be used with other forms to charms, earrings and larger pendant pieces, the possibilities are endless.

In this chapter, the use of shells to create a pair of earrings will be covered and the technique employed is a very cost effective use of silver clay. These earrings can also be made as solid forms which would be heavier and more expensive to produce.

SHELL EARRINGS

These delicate shell earrings are always popular and make great gifts. They use a surprisingly small amount of clay and, being double-sided, they can hang either way.

Tools and Materials

- 7g silver metal clay
- A small shell
- Two part silicon moulding compound
- Hand drill
- Jump rings
- Ear wires

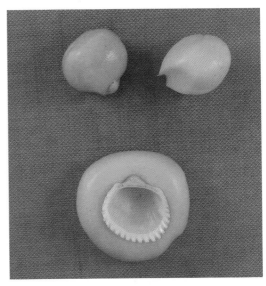

1. Make a mould of the shell.

1 Make a mould of the shell by mixing an equal quantity of each colour moulding compound together, placing the fully mixed compound in a ball on a flat surface and pushing the shell into the ball until it just comes up to the edges of the shell. Leave the shell in place and allow the mould to set – test by poking a cocktail stick into the compound.

OPPOSITE PAGE: **Jewellery made with moulds. (Photo: Paul Mounsey)**

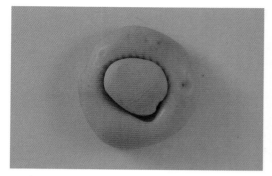

2. The patty should be about the size of the top of the mould.

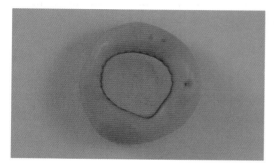

3. The patty should not come over the edges of the mould.

4. Press the shell down to texture the upper surface.

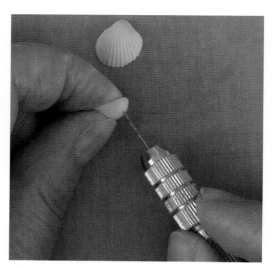

6. Apply no pressure when you drill and support from behind.

2   Take about half of the silver clay and form it into a flat patty about 2mm thick. This patty should be about the size of the top of the shell mould. Press the centre of the patty down into the mould using a finger. Try to avoid stretching the clay as this can result in the patty being too thin.

3   Press the patty against the sides of the mould moving up the sides but not coming over the edge. If the clay comes over the edge of the mould impression, too much clay has been used so start again.

4   While the clay is still moist, press the shell into the surface of the clay inside the mould making an impression of the shell on the upper surface. Do not push too hard, just gently roll the shell around the surface to get a good impression. Leave the clay to dry in the mould for best results.

5   When the clay is dry, pop it out of the mould. If the moulding has been done correctly, there should be no refining necessary. If any of the edges are ragged or flat, use a diamond file to

create a shell-like texture to the edge but do not file any of the edges flat – this spoils the organic nature of the finished item.

6   Make another piece the same and when both are fully dry, drill a hole in each one for a jump ring. Use a hand drill for this. Support the shell from behind while drilling. Apply no pressure; allow the drill bit to do the work. As long as dust is appearing as the drill turns, the hole is being made. Fire the earrings using a torch or kiln. Polish and hang on ear wires using the jump rings.

Troubleshooting

Mould lacks definition

Choose items for moulding carefully so they have good definition in the texture. Some things have good shapes but lack a defined texture so always run a finger over the surface of the item to check that there is some texture if that is important to the design. Adding a texture to the surface of moulded items which lack texture can be achieved by carving into them or using paste on the surface.

Metal clay sticks in the mould

Some items have microscopic hairs or very rough surfaces which result in moulds that stick. Unfortunately this is not always obvious until the mould is used. If sticking occurs when attempting to pop wet clay out of a mould, either scrape it out and start again with an oiled mould or leave it to dry. When the clay is completely dry it should pop out more easily. Make a note on the back of the mould with a Sharpie pen as a reminder that it requires oiling.

Edges of moulded items are not defined

Using too much clay in the mould, especially when using the double-sided mould technique described in this chapter, results in poorly defined edges or lumpy edges with no shell texture. It can take several goes to get just the right amount of clay to line the mould successfully so do not be afraid to remove the clay and start again. Make sure the clay is rehydrated between goes or use fresh clay as the technique is practised. It is worth spending time to get this technique right as it creates a realistic shell design when done properly.

Mould is too rigid

Some items which are quite deep require moulds which are rigid when fully set. These can be tricky to extract the clay from while it is still wet as it is not possible to flex them in the same way as a

Examples of deep, rigid moulds.

flatter, wider mould. Squeezing the mould can help to loosen the clay from the inside. Squeeze all the way around and then tap the mould on a hard flat surface to pop the clay out. If this does not help, once the clay is dry it should come out easily as the clay shrinks slightly during drying.

Take care not to make holes in the bottom of deep moulds.

Moulded item comes through the bottom of the mould

This normally happens when too little moulding compound has been used for the mould or if the moulding compound has started out too flat. Always use a piece of moulding compound about twice the size of the item. Estimate this by taking a piece of one colour compound that is the same size as the item to mould, then taking an equal amount of the other colour. When the compound is fully mixed, roll it into a smooth ball and press the item into the ball allowing it to spread as the item is pressed down. Pushing the sides of the moulding compound up around the item can also help to avoid the item coming through the bottom. When moulding a particularly deep item, start out with an upright sausage of moulding compound and press the item down into the end of this.

Examples of Moulded Jewellery

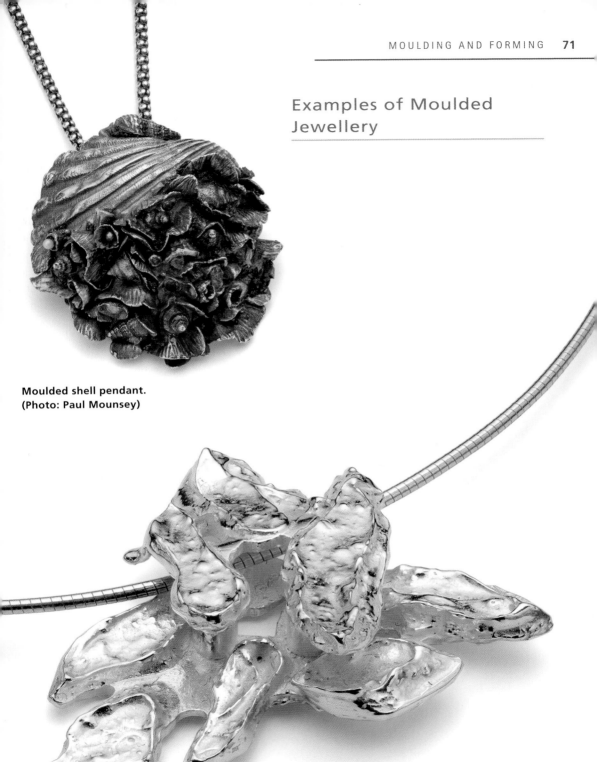

Moulded shell pendant. (Photo: Paul Mounsey)

Moulded pendant. (Photo: Paul Mounsey)

STONE SETTING

As metal clay has to be fired, the choice of stones to use in metal clay designs is limited to those which can be fired in place. Luckily, there are a wide range of man-made stones which can be fired in place and some natural stones are also safe to fire at lower temperatures. Non-fireable stones can be added to metal clay designs by using traditional silver working techniques like bezel setting.

This chapter will cover the use of fire-in-place stones, bezel setting non-fireable stones and using glass cabochons with metal clay.

Choosing and buying stones

Always buy from a source which understands metal clay when buying stones to fire in place. All the metal clay suppliers sell stones which can be fired and usually they give a firing tempera-ture which the stones have been tested for.

The most common stones sold for firing in place are cubic zirconia. These are created in a laboratory – often called lab-made stones – and are normally faceted. They come in a wide vari-ety of colours, sizes and cuts, the cut making some of them very sparkly indeed. Always check

OPPOSITE PAGE: **Jewellery with stones and glass. (Photo: Paul Mounsey)**

with the supplier about the temperature and time the stones have been tested for. The most common issue with firing cubic zirconia in place is the stone changing colour and green stones can be particularly prone to this. If in doubt, before setting the stones put them in the kiln on a piece of fibre blanket and fire them using the firing schedule intended to be used for the final piece. This shows how they will behave during firing and allows for weeding out any that do not react well.

Natural stones which can be fired in place include sapphires, rubies, garnets, moonstones, sunstones, peridot, tanzanite, alexandrite and hematite. There are a wide variety of resources on the internet which explore the firing issues with natural stones and it is always worth look-ing these up before experimenting. Some natu-ral stones will burn or explode so check before using them.

Cabochons and faceted stones

Most people are familiar with faceted stones. They are flat on the top, widen to a girdle then go in to a pointed bottom. They have multiple flat facets which reflect light and give them their characteristic sparkle. Faceted stones come in a variety of shapes including round, square, star-shaped, pear or teardrop-shaped, oval, heart-shaped, trillion – a soft triangular shape, marquise – a long oval with pointed ends, baguette – a rectangular shape, and many more.

Cabochons and faceted stones.

Cabochons are flat on the bottom and curve over in a dome shape. Some curve from the base, others have straight sides with a slightly domed top. They come in a wide variety of shapes and sizes. Natural stone cabochons can also include a 'druzy' element. This is a sparkly effect created by tiny crystals which form over the top of minerals.

Glass cabochons can be fired in place but only using a kiln. The nature of glass requires a slow heating up and cooling down phase, called 'ramping' when it is done in a programmable kiln. Heating glass up too quickly or rapid cooling results in thermal shock and the glass will crack. This is why torch firing is not suitable for metal clay pieces with glass embedded.

TIPS FOR FACETED STONE SETTING

There are some rules which need to be followed to ensure successful stone setting when using faceted stones:

The stone needs to be set far enough down so the flat top of the stone – the table – is level with the surface of the clay. During firing, the clay will shrink, gripping the stone around the widest part, the girdle, and it will draw back

from the top of the stone revealing the facets but ensuring that the stone is firmly held.

The clay the stone is set into needs to be thick enough so the point of the stone does not poke out of the back. The depth of the stone is proportionate to the size of the stone so larger stones are deeper and therefore require thicker clay to hold them securely without poking out of the back.

All metal clay dust and paste needs to be cleaned off the stone before firing. Dust and paste will fire onto the surface of the stone if it is left, making the stone cloudy and dull. Use a clean, dry brush to remove dust. A cocktail stick will remove dry paste without scratching the stone. A cotton bud dipped in alcohol will also clean the stone but do not use water; this will just add more wet metal clay to the surface of the stone.

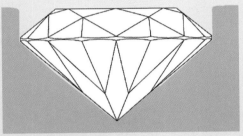

Setting a faceted stone. (Grey area is metal clay)

Setting a cubic zirconia stone in metal clay

The easiest way of setting a fireable stone in metal clay, especially a faceted cubic zirconia, is to simply push it into the wet clay. This will displace clay around the stone and can lead to an uneven and rough looking setting but it is very simple.

Another way of setting the stone is to make a hole using a drinking straw or similar cutter which is slightly smaller than the size of the stone. This takes out a plug of clay, avoiding the displacement of clay, and is a more elegant way of setting the stone. If the hole is slightly too large, putting some paste into the hole should hold the stone in place while it dries.

The cleanest and most elegant way of setting a round stone is to drill a hole for it in the dry clay. Drill a pilot hole right where the point of the stone will be. This can be drilled

all the way through or just down into the clay. Widen the hole out using progressively larger drill bits or setting burrs, constantly testing to make sure the hole is wide and deep enough for the stone to sit in but not becoming too wide. If this is done correctly in a flat piece, the stone should just sit in the hole and not require any paste to hold it there. If the piece is three-dimensional, some paste may be required to hold the stone in place.

Stone set earrings

These simple earrings are so quick and easy to make. The inclusion of fire in placing cubic zirconia allows for multiple colours to match any outfit and they can easily be made in an hour.

1. Roll a texture and cut the two earring shapes.

Tools and Materials

- 7g silver metal clay
- 2 x 3mm cubic zirconia
- Textures and a cutter
- Small drinking straw
- Drill bits 1mm, 2mm, 3mm
- Ear wires

1   Roll out the metal clay five cards thick onto a shallow texture, roll a texture into the surface and cut the two earring shapes. If the cutter shape is asymmetrical, remember to flip the cutter to get a mirror image pair. Also pay attention to the direction of the texture to ensure each earring matches in every way. Make a hole for the ear wire in each earring with a drinking straw. Put these to dry.

2   Refine the edges of each earring and refine the hole for the ear wires with a cocktail stick. Draw a dot on each earring where the stone will be set. Check carefully that they are in exactly the same place on each earring. Using a 1mm drill bit, drill a pilot hole all the way through the earrings where the stones will be.

3   Widen the top of the hole using the 2mm drill bit but do not go all the way through this time. Finally use the 3mm drill bit to make the hole wide enough for the stone to sit in but again, be careful not to go all the way through. Keep checking the size of the hole by putting the stone into the hole. The stone needs to sit right down into the hole so when looking across the surface of the earring the stone is not sticking up.

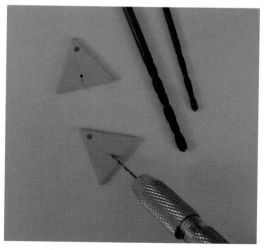

2. Drill a pilot hole for the stone in each earring.

4   Extrude a tiny amount of syringe clay into the hole and seat the stone down so it stays in place; check it is level. Allow to dry. Clean any paste or dust off the surface of the stone. When the stones are set in both earrings, lay them flat on a kiln shelf or firing block and fire. Kiln fire at 800°C/1470°F for 30 minutes or follow the instructions from the stone supplier. If the stones are torch fireable, fire for the time recommended by the stone supplier.

5   Brush or tumble to polish the earrings and add the ear wires. Triangle or star shapes can be tricky to put onto normal ear wires unless jump rings are used as the hole needs to be quite far down the point to work. Try using earring hoops for any shapes that have a hole further down.

3. Widen the hole with the 2mm and 3mm drill bits.

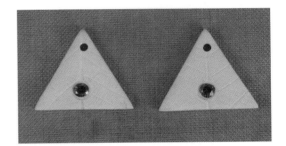

4. Earrings ready for firing.

5. Add the ear wires.

BEZEL SET PENDANT

This pendant will have a main back piece and a smaller layer into which the bezel will be embedded. This technique overcomes some of the issues associated with embedding bezel wire into metal clay and is also more economical in terms of metal clay usage.

1. Leave some space around the stone.

Tools and Materials

- 10g silver metal clay
- Overlay paste
- Cabochon
- Fine silver bezel wire
- Tweezers
- Fine-tipped marker pen
- Sharp scissors
- Textures and cutters
- Small drinking straw
- Dental floss
- Burnisher

2. Cut the bezel wire completely square to the edges.

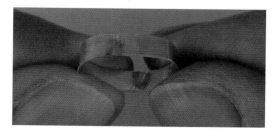

3. Push the wire slightly past itself to produce tension in the wire.edges.

1   Bend the bezel wire around the stone so it is very slightly larger than the stone. The join of the wire should be on the long edge of the oval stone. Check the size by lifting the bezel wire off the stone with tweezers; if the stone lifts at the same time, the bezel is too tight. Turn the bezel wire over frequently during this process as it is easy to push the top of the bezel wire in so the sides are not completely perpendicular.

2   When the bezel is the right size around the stone, mark the point where the bezel wire crosses itself using a fine-tipped marker pen. Cut the bezel wire to size using sharp scissors. Take care to make the cut completely square to the edges of the wire to give a good butt join for the ends of the wire.

3   Reform the bezel wire around the stone to check the size and shape again. Push the wire together slightly past itself and then open it out so the ends of the wire butt together. The

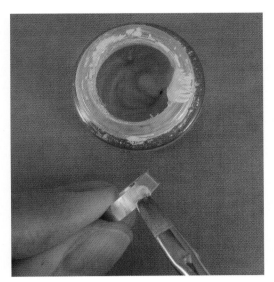

4. Paint Overlay Paste on the join.

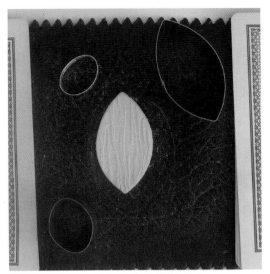

5. Cut the textured back shape.

tension of the wire should hold the join together. Check the size and shape again and correct if necessary.

4 Paint some Overlay Paste on the join inside and outside. Make sure there are no lumps of paste on the join or this will make it harder to set the stone and may prevent the stone from setting properly. Dry, then quickly torch fire the paste to set it in place, a couple of minutes will do. Check the shape of the bezel after firing to make sure it is still correct.

5 Choose an overall shape for the pendant and also a smaller shape for the layer. Make sure the layer shape is around 3mm larger than the bezel all around. Roll out the clay four cards thick onto a shallow texture and also use a shallow texture on the top surface. Cut the pendant shape, punch a jump ring hole with a straw and then, after drying, refine the edges and the jump ring hole.

6 Roll out some more clay four cards thick and cut out the layer piece. Dampen the surface of the base piece where the layer will go and

6. Stick the layer onto the back piece.

apply some paste to the back of the layer. Gently press this down onto the back piece making sure it sticks down all round. Clean up any paste that squeezes out with a damp paint-brush.

7 While the clay layer is still wet, gently push the bezel into the clay until it stops. Make sure it is level all round and adjust as necessary. Put it to dry. Once it is dry, check for any further

7. Press the bezel down until it stops.

8. Capture the stone in four places.

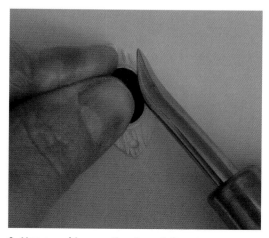

9. Use a rocking motion to set the stone.

refining that needs to be done, taking care not to damage the bezel. Fire the pendant in the kiln (900°C/1650°F for two hours) or torch/stove top fire.

8   Lay a piece of dental floss across the bezel and push the stone in to check the fit. The dental floss will allow the stone to be removed after checking if necessary. Push it right down into the bezel so it is flat and at an equal height all the way round. Remove the dental floss and push the bezel in to capture the stone on the compass points, north, south, east and west using a burnisher or bezel rocker. This holds the stone in place.

9   Hold the stone firmly in place. Use a rocking motion to push the bezel wire against the stone all the way around. Be careful not to scratch the surface of the stone, especially when setting a very soft stone. Do not overdo this rocking and pushing as this can cause the edges of the bezel to become thin and sharp. The stone should be held firmly without any movement.

10 Polish the pendant using a tumble polisher or a rotary tool with radial bristles. Tumble the pendant on its own to avoid having anything bump into the stone and damage it.

GLASS AND METAL CLAY PENDANT

Glass and silver clay work well together. Setting glass can be very economical as a relatively small amount of clay can be used to hold the glass in place on the flat back piece.

Tools and Materials

- 10g silver metal clay
- Silver clay paste
- 10–12mm glass cabochon
- Shallow textures and cutters
- Large drinking straw
- 1mm drill
- Tweezers
- Paintbrush

1   Choose a glass cabochon and design the pendant, making sure there is enough room for the glass to be securely held all around. Roll out the clay four cards thick onto a shallow texture and texture the front with a shallow texture too. Cut out the pendant shape and also cut a hole in the pendant where the cabochon will go. This hole needs to be a little smaller than the cabochon. Put it to dry.

1. Put a hole in the pendant smaller than the cabochon.

2   While the pendant is drying, make some small balls. These will be used to hold the glass in place. To make balls all the same size, roll out some clay three cards thick and use a small cutter or drinking straw to cut a number of discs. Keep these moist by covering them in cling film.

3   Take a cut out disc and roll it into a ball. Drop it into a metal saucer or tin lid to contain the balls. Take another disc from under the cling film and make another ball. Continue to make balls in this way until all the discs are used. It is always good to make more than immediately needed as these keep well and are useful to add embellishment to future creations. Put these aside to dry.

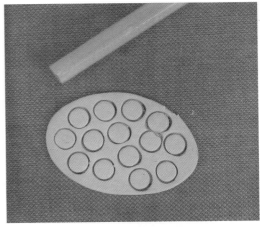

2. Cut out a number of small circles to make balls.

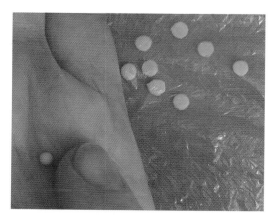

3. Roll the circle into a ball.

4. Stick a ball to the pendant up against the cabochon.

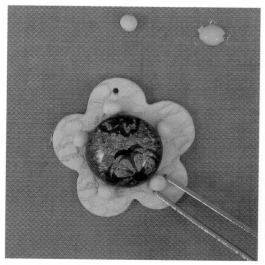

5. Stick balls all around the cabochon.

4   Refine the pendant edges and the inside of the hole. Drill a 1mm hole for a jump ring. Lay the pendant on a flat surface and put the cabochon in place. Dispense a small amount of paste onto the work mat. Pick up a ball using tweezers and dip it into the paste. Stick this to the surface of the pendant, up against the cabochon on one side. Make sure the paste is stuck to the surface of the pendant, not the glass. Clean any excess paste with a damp paintbrush.

5   Stick another ball on the other side of the cabochon in a position which is pleasing to the overall design, then another between the two balls and another on the opposite side. Clean up excess paste as each ball is placed. Continue adding balls until the cabochon is held in place. Put this to dry.

6   If the balls are large enough to hold the cabochon firmly in place after firing, stop there. They need to come up the cabochon beyond the point where it curves in. Remember that they will shrink during the firing but the glass will not. If they are too small to hold it in place, add more balls. Pile them up or arrange them all around the cabochon.

6. Add more balls to hold the cabochon.

7 When everything is dry, clean all paste or dust off the glass with a dry brush. Any paste or dust on the glass will fire to it. Pieces that combine glass and metal clay can only be fired in the kiln as glass needs to heat up and cool down slowly to avoid thermal shock. Set the kiln to ramp at 800°C/1470°F per hour rising to 700°C/1290°F and hold for 30 minutes. When the firing is over, leave the kiln door closed until the temperature has dropped to 40°C/104°F.

8 Polish the pendant by brass brushing gently in soapy water. This can be tumble polished on its own to avoid having things bump into the glass and damage it. Alternatively use a power tool with radial bristle brushes. Add a jump ring.

8. Polish the pendant with radial brushes.

ALTERNATIVE WAYS OF HOLDING A GLASS CABOCHON IN PLACE

There are many ways of holding a glass cabochon in place in a metal clay design. The main rule of thumb is that the cabochon should be held in three places or in a C shape. Check that the cabochon cannot fall out, either to one side or from the top if the holding mechanism is not high enough.

Balls all round
This configuration works if the balls are large enough to come up the sides of the cabochon sufficiently to hold it in.

Balls on three points
Again, this works if the balls are large enough to hold the cabochon firmly enough.

Balls in a C shaped configuration
Make sure the balls come around the cabochon enough not to allow it to drop out of the side. They also need to be large enough to hold the cabochon in at the top.

Snakes
A long snake shape can be used to hold the cabochon either to the side in a C shape, all around the base or over the top. Roll the snake using a flat piece of acrylic, like a CD case and use it wet so it drapes around or over the cabochon. Make sure it is high enough to hold the cabochon in.

Discs
The discs that are cut out to make the balls can also be used to hold the cabochon in place. These are normally best used wet rather than being allowed to dry like the balls. This makes them trickier to use but they can be very effective.

Any combination of snakes, discs and balls can be used.

Flowers, leaves, hearts
Very small cutters can produce shapes to hold the cabochon in place. Tiny flowers, leaves, hearts or any other shape cut from clay two cards thick and used wet add interest to the piece or continue a theme used for the main design. Follow the rules and have some fun with the design.

Troubleshooting

The faceted stone is not straight

Once the piece is fired, there is nothing to be done about this. Always check carefully before firing the piece to make sure the stone is straight. Hold it up to a light source and tilt it to one side slightly watching the light bounce off the table of the stone. This should show if the stone is level. If it is not, poke it out from the back (if a pilot hole has been drilled all the way through) and reset it.

Sometimes if the aperture for the stone is too big or has been drilled at an angle, this can result in the stone not sitting level. Add some paste down into the hole and bed the stone down into this, levelling it up. Allow it to dry, clean off excess paste and check it again before firing.

The cubic zirconia has changed colour

This can happen if the stone has come from a source that does not understand firing cubic zirconias in metal clay or if the suggested firing schedule has not been followed. A cubic zirconia can be drilled out using a glass drill bit in a bench drill with the drilling done under water but it is risky and not to be attempted without the proper precautions. Always test stones before setting them, especially if they have been bought from an untested source.

The bezel is too high for the cabochon

If the cabochon sits right down inside the bezel, during the setting process there will be wrinkling of the bezel as it is being pushed too far over the stone. Raise the stone up by adding a piece of copper wire bent to fit around the inside bottom

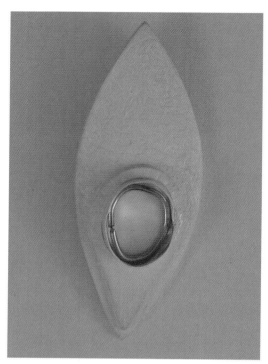

A piece of copper wire in the bottom of the bezel.

of the bezel. The gauge of wire used will depend on how much too high the bezel is. Add the copper wire to the bottom of the bezel and set the stone on top of this.

The bezel is visible or has come right through the back of the pendant

This occurs when the bezel wire is pushed too far into the wet clay or when the clay has been rolled out too thinly. It can be covered up by adding lump clay or thick paste to the back of the freshly fired piece, drying and refiring.

Puckering of the clay behind the bezel

This normally occurs in pieces which are made too thin. As the silver clay is shrinking, the bezel wire – which is solid and not shrinking – causes resistance and stress, resulting in this puckering. Making a hole through the whole piece inside the bezel wire can help to reduce this stress. This hole can also add a decorative element to the back of the piece after the stone is set. Making the whole piece thicker or embedding the bezel wire in a layer on top of the back piece can also help to prevent this. There is not much that can be done about it once the piece is fired although if it is very unsightly, adding thick paste or fresh clay to the puckered area and refiring it can cover it up.

Puckering on the back.

The bezel is too big for the stone

This becomes obvious when testing the fit of the stone in the bezel and results in a lot of movement of the stone inside the bezel. This can result in wrinkles in the bezel when setting the stone. Unless a better fitting stone can be found, there is not much that can be done about this.

The join in the bezel bursts

This normally occurs when testing the stone in the bezel and suggests that the bezel is too small for the stone. Find a smaller stone which fits better if possible. The join can be repasted and fired again. An alternative is to make a V cut in the bezel where the join was, creating a feature at that point. As long as the stone is securely held when it is set, the join being open will not cause any problems.

There is a yellow or green/grey halo where the glass and silver clay touch

Glass will react with the silver if it is fired at too high a temperature. If the glass begins to soften and flow, it will react with the silver and produce a halo effect where the two meet. This varies in colour depending on the glass used. Keep the temperature at or under 700°C/1290°F and fire for no more than 30 minutes to avoid this.

Using Bullseye Crystal Clear glass as the top layer of the fusing stack when making glass cabochons will also help to reduce reactions between the silver and the glass.

Examples of Stone Set Jewellery

Hollow brooch with stones.
(Photo: Paul Mounsey)

Brooch with multiple stone settings.
(Photo: Paul Mounsey)

3D necklace with Oregon sunstone.
(Photo: Paul Mounsey)

RING MAKING

Making rings with metal clay presents a couple of problems which need to be considered. Firstly, the shrinkage of the metal clay has to be accounted for when making a ring in order for it to fit. Secondly, because rings are worn on the hand, they can get quite a bit of hard wear. As fine silver is softer than Sterling, there is the potential for the ring to become misshapen over time. If the ring is not fired long and hot in the kiln, it can also be prone to breakage so generally, torch firing is not suitable for metal clay rings, especially if they are going to be worn regularly.

There are several other things that can affect the final size of the ring besides accounting for the shrinkage. If the ring is a little loose around the mandrel, this can result in the ring being a bit too big. If lots of sanding inside the ring is required during the dry stage, this can also affect the size of the ring. Generally, ring making requires some practice and experimentation to find out which combination of techniques results in an accurate final size consistently. Once this is established, use that process to achieve consistent results.

Accounting for Shrinkage

There are two main ways to account for the shrinkage of metal clay when making rings; mathematical calculation and using a ring sizer.

Mathematical calculation

Metal clay shrinks by around 10 per cent to 15 per cent depending on the brand used so by increasing the size of the ring band by this amount, after shrinkage the ring should be the right size.

The process for this is as follows:

Measure the size of the finger using a tape measure and note down the length in millimetres. Multiply the length by 0.1 or 0.15 to find out the length of a 10 per cent or 15 per cent increase in the length. Add the two figures together to find out the length of the ring band required before firing.

Here is an example when using PMC3:
Finger size = 60mm
60 x 0.15 = 9mm this is 15 per cent of 60mm
Pre-firing ring size = finger size + 15 per cent
= 69mm

OPPOSITE PAGE: **Metal clay rings.**
(Photo: Paul Mounsey)

Using a ring sizer

Ring sizers are different depending on which country's sizer is used. Some also have half sizes as well as full sizes so be aware of this when buying one. Choose a ring sizer and stick to it when making metal clay rings. It actually does not matter which country's sizer is used as long as it is used consistently. Thicker and wider rings shrink more as do larger sized rings. The more clay is used, the more shrinkage will result. Also the method of firing will affect the shrinkage. Long hot firing will result in more shrinkage than torch firing. When starting to make rings, experiment, find out what works and stick to it.

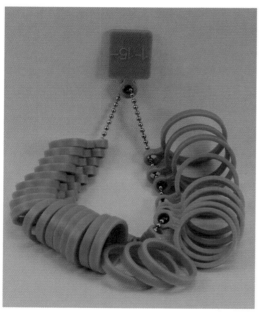

Ring sizers.

UK ring sizers

For rings up to 5mm wide, add 2 to 2.5 sizes. Heavy rings up to 20mm wide and/or thicker than six cards may need 2.5 to 4.5 sizes added.

Japanese ring sizers

For rings up to 3mm wide, use a size 2 to 3 times larger than the size needed. For rings around 5mm wide, use a size 3 times larger. For a ring which is 10mm wide or thicker than five cards, make it 4 to 5 sizes larger.

US ring sizers

For rings up to 5mm wide, add 1 to 1.25 sizes. Heavy rings up to 20mm wide and/or thicker than six cards may need 1.5 to 2 sizes added.

OPEN BAND RING

This type of ring is the simplest to make but it does require a kiln to fire. The ring is made as a long flat band and fired flat, then bent around a steel mandrel after firing. In order for it to stand up to the bending process after firing, it requires a long, hot firing in the kiln.

Tools and Materials

- 10g silver clay
- Teflon
- Small cutters for embellishment
- Textures
- Emery board
- Steel mandrel
- Rawhide or nylon mallet
- Slim bristled brass/steel brush
- Normal brass/steel brush

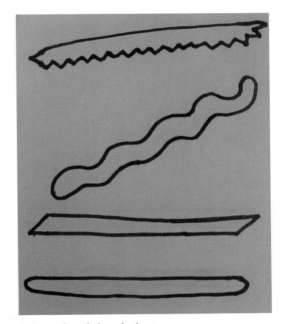

1. Open band ring designs.

1   Take some time to think about the design. This type of ring allows for designs which include an opening at the front or the back, blunt or pointed ends, slanted ends or rings which wrap around the finger more than once. Bypass rings can also be made which bend around the finger at an angle.

2   Make a paper template of the design to size including the mathematical calculation for shrinkage. If it is going to be a bypass ring, make sure there is enough extra length to accommodate the amount of cross over the design calls for.

3   Prepare a long piece of Teflon, adding oil along the length. Roll the clay into a long, thin sausage shape and then roll this down to five cards thick. When using playing cards, these will need to be moved during rolling as it is likely that the length of the ring will be longer than the cards.

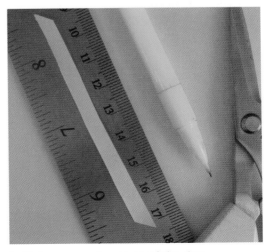

2. Make a paper template of the ring.

4   Texture the surface of the ring and then use a straight blade to cut it to the width the design requires. Trim the ends to the length of the paper template. Put the ring to dry, making sure it is straight.

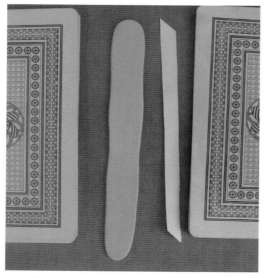

3. Roll a sausage of clay down to five cards thick.

5   Carefully refine the edges and ends of the dry ring. The easiest way to do this is to put an emery board flat down on the table and run the ring length along it on each side. The longer the ring length is, the more prone to breaking it is. If it breaks, rehydrate the clay and start again, even if it is well fixed, this will be a weak spot when it is bent around the mandrel later.

6   Roll out the excess clay cut out the embellishments and put these to dry. When the embellishments are dry, refine them and then stick them firmly onto the ring using thick paste. As this ring will be bent around the mandrel after firing, embellishments need to be stuck on really well to avoid them popping off later.

7   When the ring is completely dry, put it onto a kiln shelf and fire at 900°C/1650°F for two hours. After firing, bend the ring around a steel mandrel, starting at one end of the band and moving slowly along the length, bending each part close to the last bend.

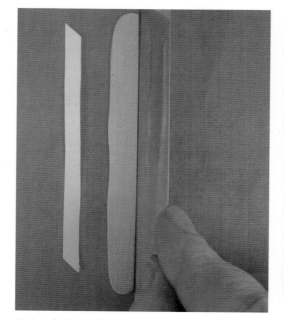

4. Cut the length with a straight blade.

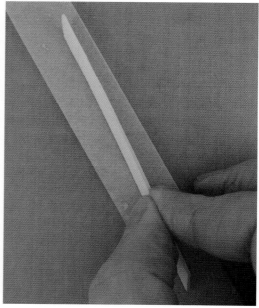

5. Refine the edges of the ring.

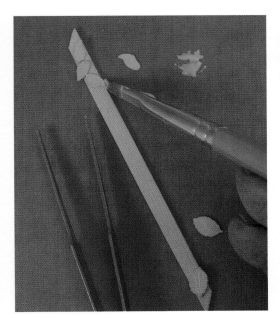

6. Stick embellishments onto the ring.

7. Bend the fired ring around the mandrel.

8. Use a mallet to bend the final piece of the band.

9. Polish the inside with a slim brush.

8 If the ring is going to be a bypass, start the bending at an angle. Keep thumbs close together as the ring is bent and pay attention to the size. At the end of the process, the metal can become too hard to bend by hand. Use a mallet to tap the final piece into shape against the mandrel.

9 Polish the inside of the ring using a slim bristled brush and the outside with a normal brush. Tumble polish or hand polish the embellishments to achieve the desired finish.

CONTINUOUS BAND RING

This ring is constructed on a wooden mandrel from a rolled out length of clay. It can be textured or plain, pierced or have stones set into the band. It also looks good with syringe decoration.

1. Draw lines on the mandrel where the ring will be formed.

2. Stick greaseproof paper around the mandrel.

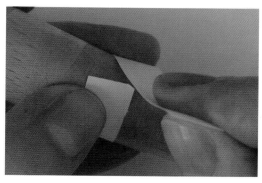

3. Measure how long the clay needs to be.

Tools and Materials

- 10–15g silver clay
- Thick silver clay paste
- Silver clay syringe
- Straight blade
- Greaseproof paper
- Sticky tape
- Wooden mandrel and stand
- Sanding pads
- Sandpaper 400–600 grit
- Slim bristled brass/steel brush
- Normal brass/steel brush

1   Use the ring sizers to determine the size of the ring taking into account the shrinkage. Slide the appropriate sized ring form onto the mandrel and draw a line each side on the mandrel using a pencil. This will be where the ring is formed.

2   Cut a piece of greaseproof paper long enough to wrap around the mandrel where the mark is. Stick the edges of this down with sticky tape so it stays in place. The lines should be visible through the paper.

3   Wrap another piece of paper around the mandrel and mark where they meet to determine the minimum length the clay needs to be rolled out to. Add on at least 2cm to this length as the ends of the clay need to be overlapping when they are wrapped round the mandrel.

4   Roll the clay into a long slim sausage and then roll this down to five cards thick. Use a straight blade to cut the length of clay into a band

4. Cut the rolled out clay into a band.

5. Flap the ends over each other.

5mm wide but do not trim the ends. Lightly dampen the length of the clay; this will help it to stick to the paper around the mandrel.

5   Pick up the length of clay and wrap it around the mandrel, damp side down, exactly over the lines visible through the paper. One end should flap over the other. Cut down through both layers at a 45° angle and discard the excess from the top and underneath.

6   Flap the top layer back and put a generous amount of thick paste down on the paper and up the join. Gently press the top layer down onto the pasted join, making sure not to squash the band. Ensure the top of the band makes a continuous line over the join and the two ends are in contact.

7   Leave the ring on the mandrel to dry. It is not unusual for the join to pop open slightly during drying. If this happens, once it is dry, before removing it from the mandrel, use well hydrated lump clay or syringe to fill any gaps in the join and allow this to dry.

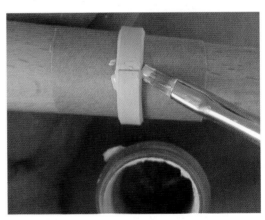

6. Join the two ends with paste.

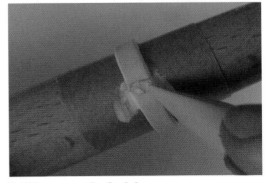

7. Fill any gaps in the join.

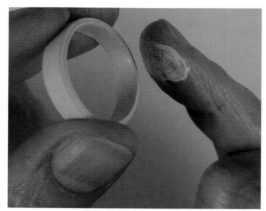

8. Use a wet finger to smooth the inside of the join.

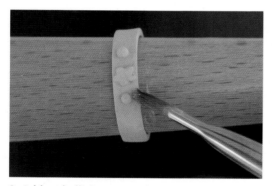

9. Add embellishment to the ring.

8   When the ring is dry, slide the paper off the mandrel and remove it from the inside of the ring by gently twisting it away from the band all around. Fill in any gaps on the inside of the join with hydrated lump clay or syringe and dry again. Run a wet finger over the join on the inside of the ring and dry. Do the same for the outside join and dry.

9   Sand the edges of the ring flat down on sandpaper and use sanding pads if necessary on the inside and outside. Add embellishment or texture using paste or syringe. Dry and fire, preferably in a kiln at 900°C/1650°F for two hours. Flat band rings should be put on a bed of fibre blanket or vermiculite to prevent drag on the kiln shelf. Polish.

ADDING PEARLS AND HALF-DRILLED BEA

Pearls and semi-precious half-drilled beads will not stand up to firing so they have to be added after firing. They work well in rings but can also be added to any jewellery items.

Plan where the pearl or bead will go on the design and make sure to account for shrinkage of the clay during firing, especially when planning to put the pearl inside an aperture rather than standing proud from the surface.

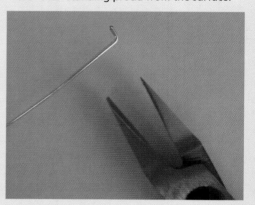

Bend a small L in the wire.

When using fine silver metal clay, embedding a piece of fine silver wire which fits the hole in the pearl or bead is the easiest way to set them. Take a piece of fine silver wire and bend a small L shape onto one end. Use a longer length of wire than is actually needed so it is easy to hold and place, it will be cut to the correct length after firing.

While the clay is still moist, embed the wire into the clay where the pearl/bead will go. Stab the end of the L down into the clay and then pull the wire up so it is perpendicular to the surface of the clay. Clean up the surface of the clay, making sure the wire is securely held and put the piece to dry.

Once the piece is dry, make sure the wire is still held firmly. If it is loose or wobbly, add some syringe into the hole but make sure there is no paste up the wire as this will prevent the pearl/bead from sitting all the way down onto the wire. The ideal end result is for the pearl/bead

Stab the end down into the clay.

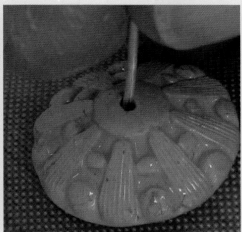

Pull the wire up.

to appear to be floating on the surface of the silver so it needs to be pushed right down on the wire.

It is often easier to make pieces which combine a wire for a pearl/bead in component parts, like a ring with a moulded topper. Make the ring band, dry and refine it. Make the topper and embed the wire in the wet stage, dry and refine. Then stick the topper to the ring band when they are both dry. This allows easy handling but take care not to dislodge the wire when sticking the two pieces together. Make sure the two pieces fit together well with a good contact point. If necessary, file a flat platform on the ring band and on the base of the topper piece so there is good surface to surface contact. A clothes peg is a useful tool to gently hold the ring band steady and upright while sticking the topper on. It can also help to keep the piece upright during drying. Use very thick paste or syringe to stick them together as this creates a stronger bond than thin paste. Stick the topper over the join in the ring band to make the ring even stronger.

After firing, polish the piece. The final step is to stick the pearl/bead on. Cut the wire down in stages, checking that the pearl/bead fits on. Cut small pieces off the wire until the pearl/bead just sits on top of the silver surface. Be careful not to cut the wire too short; the longer

the wire is up inside the pearl/bead, the more secure it will be.

Use two-part epoxy glue, jewellery glue or a cyanoacrylate glue to stick the pearl/bead onto the wire. Put a small amount of glue on the top of the wire and run the half-drilled pearl/bead up and down the wire, twisting it around so the glue coats the inside of the hole and wire. If there is any excess glue on the silver, clean it off immediately. Allow it to dry following the glue manufacturer's guidelines.

Make the component parts separately.

Troubleshooting

Breakage before firing

If a ring breaks during the making process, it will always be weak, no matter how good the fix is. The best idea is to crush the clay up and rehydrate, then make the ring again. Breaks can be fixed with paste but if any hammering needs to be done after firing, this will most likely cause breakage, no matter how well the ring has been fired.

Breakage after firing

If a ring breaks after firing there may be several causes. If the ring was broken and fixed during the making process, this will result in a weak spot. The area of the join is always going to be a weak spot on a ring so if embellishment is being added, putting this over the join area will help to make that spot stronger.

Torch firing for three minutes is fine for a ring which will only be worn occasionally and/or with very light wear. It is not sufficient for a ring which will be worn more often and definitely not for a ring which is going to be worn when the wearer is doing manual work. Rings should be fired long and hot in the kiln if they are going to be as strong as possible.

The ring is not round

Sometimes rings come out of the making and firing process not completely round. Fine silver rings are also prone to squashing during wear as the metal is soft. If the ring is fired directly down on a kiln shelf, friction can cause drag on the bottom edge during shrinkage, resulting in a ring with sides that are not straight.

Rings can be rounded on a steel mandrel with a rawhide or nylon mallet. Drop the ring onto the mandrel and hammer all around once. Take the ring off the mandrel, turn it around and drop it back onto the mandrel the other way around. As a steel mandrel is graduated, this prevents the ring from ending up with a graduated shape. The join in the ring is a weak spot so do not over hammer the ring. This process can tend to stretch the ring and may result in the ring breaking at the point of the join if too much hammering is done.

Size issues

Some experimentation with sizing techniques is initially required to find a method which results in consistent sizing accuracy. Rings which are a little too small can be stretched by around half a size using the rounding method with a steel mandrel and mallet. Any more than half a size and there is a risk of the ring popping open at the join.

If the ring is too big, further firing may result in additional shrinkage. An alternative is to cut the ring open with a jewellers saw, take out a small section and then make the ring an open band variety. It can also be soldered or fused closed again or use thick silver clay paste to stick it and refire.

Examples of Rings

**Starfish moulded ring topper with pearl.
(Photo: Paul Mounsey)**

**Hand moulded open band ring.
(Photo: Paul Mounsey)**

BEAD MAKING

Beads come in all shapes and sizes and can be used as components in jewellery designs or as a focal point in their own right. This chapter will explore a very simple rolled bead design and a lentil bead which is a simple hollow form construction project.

ROLLED BEAD

This bead is very simple to make and allows for multiple design possibilities. Hung on thick leather or suede cord, they appeal to men and women equally.

Tools and Materials

- 5–7g silver clay
- Silver clay paste
- Teflon
- Texture
- Large diameter drinking straw
- Craft knife

1 Oil a drinking straw. This bead is a hollow form which will wrap over itself so it can be rolled thinner than a flat piece. Roll out the clay three cards thick onto a sheet of Teflon and texture the surface.

2 Cut the clay into a long, triangular shape. The length of the triangle will dictate how many times the bead will wrap around the straw.

1. Roll the clay and texture it.

OPPOSITE PAGE: **Rolled and lentil beads.**
(Photo: Paul Mounsey)

2. Cut a long triangular shape.

3. Roll the clay around the straw.

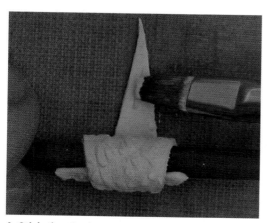

4. Stick the tip down with paste.

3 Turn the triangle over so the texture is underneath. Place the drinking straw onto the wide end of the triangle and roll the straw down the length, keeping the clay snug to the straw.

4 Put some paste on the very tip of the triangle and stick this to the body of the bead. Allow it to dry, refine the ends as necessary and fire. Polish as normal.

ROLL-OVER BAILS

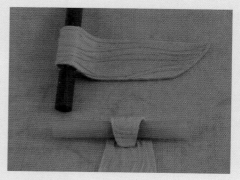

Roll-over bails.

The rolled bead design easily adapts to make a roll-over bail, one of the simplest metal clay bail techniques. Design a pendant which is long enough to accommodate an element which can be rolled over a drinking straw in the same way as the beginning of the rolled bead. Stick the end down using paste to form a very simple bail.

This bail can be made to either flap over from the back to the front or from the front to the back to make a hidden bail.

The success of the roll-over bail is in the design and often it is best to use a freeform shape rather than a cutter. Plan it on paper and cut a template which will flap over the drinking straw and stick down but still have enough of a pendant below to make it attractive.

Think carefully about how the back texture will work with the front texture when planning a bail to flap from back to front.

LENTIL BEAD

This bead is so-called due to its shape. The bead halves are dried on a domed surface and joined after drying to create the bead. The depth of the bead is dictated by the size of the circle and the form on which it is dried. Totally spherical beads can be created using this method as well as shallower beads.

Tools and Materials

- 10–15g silver clay
- Syringe or paste
- Round cutter
- Domed forms
- Texture
- Sandpaper 400–600 grit
- Files
- Drills

1. A selection of domed forms.

1 Anchor the domed forms if necessary. When using light bulbs, ping pong balls or marbles, polymer clay will hold them in place. Measuring spoons the same size also make good forms for domed beads and require no anchoring. Oil the surface of the domed forms.

2 Take half the clay and roll it out four cards thick, texture it and cut a circle. Transfer the clay to the domed form and gently press the edges down onto the form. Make sure it makes good contact with the form all round. Repeat this with the second half of the bead and allow both to air dry.

3 Put the sandpaper flat down onto the table and file the edge of one half, creating a flat platform on the edge. Move finger pressure around the form during sanding to prevent one area getting more sanding than others. Repeat with the second half.

4 The sanding should provide a flat platform on each half which can then be easily stuck

2. Put the circles onto the domed forms.

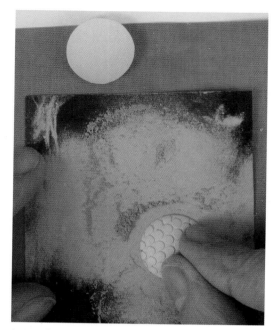

3. Sand the edge.

4. Example of the correct filing of the half.

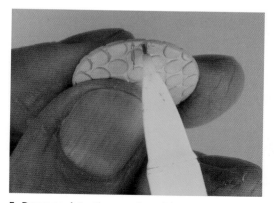

5. Draw registration marks with a pencil.

together. Be careful not to over file as this will make the bead half smaller. Equally, enough material needs to be removed so the join is neat and clean.

5   Check how the bead fits together and if there is one way it fits better than another, draw registration marks on both halves across the join with a pencil. This allows easy fitting of the two halves together at the best point.

6   Dampen the platform on each bead and then put paste or syringe all around one half. Pick up both halves; find the registration marks on each half and stick them together, lining up the marks.

7   Press the halves firmly together at the edges, leaving any paste that squeezes out and allow to dry. When they are dry, use finger nails to pick off any excess paste and make the join neat. Sand the join gently if necessary but be careful not to destroy the texture.

6. Stick both halves together.

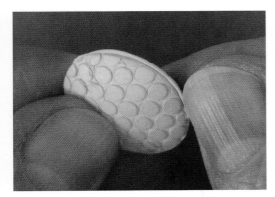

7. Pick off excess paste with finger nails.

8   Decide where the hole is going to go on the bead as this will dictate how the bead will hang. Draw pencil marks on the bead where the holes will be. Also consider the size of the holes which will depend on what it is going to hang on.

9   File a small ridge into the bead edges where the holes will be. Drill two holes in the bead, making sure that the direction of drilling points towards the other hole, not at a right angle to the edge of the bead. Holes which point into the bead will be impossible to string whereas holes which point to each other will allow a wire or chain to pass through in the right direction.

10 Widen the holes if necessary by using a larger drill or open with small files. Nestle the bead on fibre blanket or in vermiculite to support the curved shape and fire. Small beads can be fired by torch but larger beads will need kiln firing. Polish as normal.

8. Examples of bead holes.

9. Drill in the direction of the other hole.

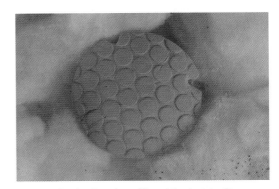

10. Nestle the bead on fibre blanket to fire.

Troubleshooting

Firing beads

Hollow forms need to be supported from underneath during firing so they do not end up with a flat area. Fibre blanket is a good option, as is vermiculite. Build the fibre blanket up so it supports the curve of the bead all round.

Occasionally a bead may collapse during firing. This is normally due to the clay being rolled out too thinly. It can also be caused by heavy embellishment on the surface of the bead. If the bead is to have heavy embellishment, make the basic bead slightly thicker so it is stronger.

Be careful about putting things inside the bead during firing. The shrinkage can be impeded by having something inside the form which can cause the seams to burst.

Size of holes

If the intention is for the bead to be hung directly on a chain, the hole needs to be large enough not just for the chain but also for the ring at the end of the chain. Consider this carefully in the dry stage when drilling the hole. If the hole is too small after firing, increase the size using a drill or gently squeeze the ring on the chain so it is oval shaped and fits through the holes.

If the bead is going to be strung with other beads or spacer beads, make sure the holes are not so big that the other beads go inside. Shrinkage always needs to be considered so, if in doubt, make the holes smaller and widen them if necessary after firing.

Polishing hollow forms

Beads with small holes that are smaller than the steel shot in a tumbler are fine but if the bead has larger holes or for rolled beads, the shot can get inside the bead during tumbling. Getting the shot out can be a long and tedious process so put something into the hole to prevent shot from getting in there. A pipe cleaner works well as does a piece of wire in smaller holes.

Brushing and burnishing are also ways of polishing beads. Polishing inside the hole can be difficult, especially in the case of the rolled bead. There are small bail brushes that work well inside the bead hole and metallic pipe cleaners also do the job. Wrapping a piece of polishing paper around a cocktail stick makes a good polishing tool for small holes.

:xamples of Beads in Jewellery

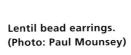

Lentil bead earrings.
(Photo: Paul Mounsey)

Pendant based on a lentil bead.
(Photo: Paul Mounsey)

SUPPLIERS

UK Suppliers

Art clay, tools, textures, cutters and materials

Metal Clay Ltd.
1–2 Omega Centre, Sandford Lane, Wareham
BH20 4DY. www.metalclay.co.uk

Creative Glass UK
11–12 Sextant Park, Neptune Close,
Medway City Estate, Rochester, Kent, ME2 4LU.
www.creativeglassshop.co.uk

PMC, tools, textures, cutters and materials

The PMC Studio
87 New Road, Weston Turville,
Buckinghamshire, HP22 5QT.
www.thepmcstudio.com

General jewellery making supplies

Cooksongold
59–83 Vittoria Street, Birmingham, B1 3NZ.
www.cooksongold.com

Palmer Metals Ltd
401 Broad Lane, Coventry CV5 7AY.
www.palmermetals.co.uk

Textures

Simply Sequins Limited
82 Durrants Road, Rowlands Castle, Hants PO9
6BG. www.simplysequins.co.uk – Punchinella

Skeleton Leaf
368 Huntington Road, York YO31 9HP. www.
skeleton-leaf.com

Cutters and stencils

Kit Box
Unit 3, Neads Court, Knowles Road, Clevedon,
North Somerset BS21 7XS. www.kitbox.co.uk

Technical Drawing Supplies
Apartment 4, The Strand, 74A Broad Road,
Sale, Cheshire M33 2ER.
www.technical-drawing.co.uk

Fine Cut Sugarcraft
Workshop 4, Old Stable Block,
Holme Pierrepont Hall, Holme Pierrepont,
Nottingham NG12 2LD.
www.finecutsugarcraft.com

Stones and Pearls

Diamond CZ
www.diamondcz.co.uk – sales@diamondcz.co.uk

Kernowcraft Rocks & Gems Ltd
Penwartha Road, Bolingey, Perranporth, Cornwall TR6 0DH.
www.kernowcraft.co.uk

Manchester Minerals
Tel: +44 (0)161 477 1151
Email: gemcraft@btconnect.com
www.manchesterminerals.co.uk

International Suppliers

Metal clay, tools, textures, cutters and materials

Cool Tools
945 N Parkway Street, Jefferson, WI 53549. www.cooltools.us

Metal Clay Supply
225 Cash Street, Jacksonville, TX 75766.
www.metalclaysupply.com

Metal Clays
US Phone: (702) 218–4928
www.metalclays.com

Art clay, tools, textures, cutters and materials

Art Clay World USA Inc.
535 Southwest Hwy, Oak Lawn, Illinois 60453.
www.artclayworld.com

PMC, tools, textures, cutters and materials

PMC Connection Inc.
PO Box 570968 Dallas, TX 75357.
www.pmcconnection.com

The PMC Studio France
Figuès, 47600 Moncrabeau, France.
www.pmcstudiofrance.com

Metal Clay Studios Germany
Email: info@metalclaystudios.de
Phone: + 49-89-12 12 99 77
www.metalclaystudios.de

General jewellery making supplies

Rio Grande
7500 Bluewater Rd NW, Albuquerque, NM 87121 USA. www.riogrande.com

Textures

Rolling Mill Resource
Minnesota, United States. www.etsy.com/shop/rollingmillresource

Barbara McGuire
USA Phone: 678-654-7055
Email: barbara@barbaramcguire.com
http://store.barbaramcguire.com

Cutters and stencils

Isomars
219 Okhla Industrial Area Phase-1 New Delhi - 20 India.
www.isomars.com

Cheap Cookie Cutters
3225 S. MacDill Ave, Suite 129-340, Tampa, FL 33629.
www.cheapcookiecutters.com

Global Sugar Art
1509 Military Turnpike, Plattsburgh, NY 12901.
www.globalsugarart.com

Stones and pearls

Fine Designer Cabochons
Jim Harman, PO Box 1733, Rogue River, OR 97537.
www.fine-designer-cabochons.com

Fire Mountain Gems
One Fire Mountain Way, Grants Pass, OR USA 97526-2373.
www.firemountaingems.com

Gem Resources
PO Box 62006, Minneapolis, MN 55426.
www.gemresources.com

SOURCES OF MORE INFORMATION

Metal Clay Academy

www.metalclayacademy.com

The Metal Clay Academy is an independent online resource listing suppliers, teachers and resources useful to metal clay artists worldwide. It is a one-stop-shop for everything to do with metal clay and a useful place to start when looking for further information about working with metal clay.

Metal Clay Masters Registry

www.mastersregistry.com

The Masters Registry is a structured program linked to an independent evaluation system that is the most prestigious and professional credential in the field of metal clay. A rigorous curriculum of fifty projects provides artists with a challenge that will propel them to improved technical skills and into new creative realms.

INDEX